GIVE UP YOUR SMALL AMBITIONS

By

Michael C. Griffiths

Accelerated Christian Education,® Inc.
Lewisville, Texas

Reprinted but not edited by

ACCELERATED CHRISTIAN EDUCATION,® INC., 1993.

ISBN 1-56265-017-3

1 2 3 4 5   Printing/Year   97 96 95 94 93

Printed in the United States of America

Contents

Tell the students to give up their small ambitions and come eastward to preach the gospel of Christ. . . .

FRANCIS XAVIER (1506-52)

Introduction

THIS BOOK almost never was. I had set aside a vacation in the Cameron Highlands of Malaysia to get it written. On the first morning of that vacation I went out for a short morning stroll with two other missionaries and my five-year-old son, intending to be back for lunch. We missed our way on the jungle path going back, and it was soon clear that we were really lost, without map, compass, matches, food, water, or warm clothing.

For nine hours we struggled along stream beds, dodged an ugly-looking pit viper, and clambered through dense jungle, I with Nigel on my back. When darkness fell we decided to settle down on a ridge for the night. Some others who had been lost had been gone for four days; other had never been found. So during those hours I was forced to think about my "just one life" afresh. What had I achieved after all? Would I ever see my wife and the other children again? What a mess for the OMF after all the bother of appointing a new General Director to lose him so soon. To know that one's life is in serious peril, and to have time to think about it, marvelously sharpens the faculties!

Looked at calmly, here were a sixty-two-year-old veteran from Tibet, two other men in their early forties, and a (fortunately) blissful five-year-old, who had stayed out rather later than intended and missed lunch and supper. "Why don't we look for a hotel?" he inquired, suspicious that this might be another bit of missionary economy! Would that it were quite so simple!

Looked at differently, would we be found? What if a tiger found us first? Or if one of us got bitten by a pit viper? What if life, that one short life, were almost over now? Were there

better ways in which it might have been used? What about
that job as leader of a large missionary society, scarcely begun?
What about my wife and the children? How would they manage?

And what about that book, still unwritten? It had been
drafted in outline two or three years earlier, in a freezing cold
village in South Korea with the ground rock-hard and the
rivers all frozen. Funny to get an idea for the title when lost
in the Malayan jungle. Perhaps I ought to have called it *Just
One Life*.

At any rate, a rescue party reached us at 10:30 that night, although another four hours of struggling through jungle and
along stream beds lay ahead, with someone else carrying Nigel.
(In retrospect it was some comfort that even our rescuers lost
the trail on the way home!) But the next day, after a long
sleep, out came the draft manuscript. Now that book could
be written.

Just one life. This is all any one of us has to offer. How can
it be used for the greatest glory of God and the greatest blessing to men? How can we be as useful as possible and as effective
as possible as Christians?

Francis Xavier was the Jesuit director of missions in India,
China, and Japan in the sixteenth century. He once said that
he longed to be back in Paris "to go shouting up and down
the streets to tell the students to give up their small ambitions
and come eastward to preach the gospel of Christ." More than
four hundred years later, my sentiments would be very similar.
Not that I think that every keen Christian worth his salt ought
to volunteer to be a foreign missionary,[1] or to become a "full-
time Christian worker."[2] But I do think that the churches and
the Christians who belong to them should face up to the need

[1]Indeed, chap. 1 makes it plain that I do not believe in our present
volunteer system at all!
[2]See the author's *Consistent Christianity* (Chicago: Inter-Varsity, n.d.),
p. 30.

of the international church all over the world far more realistically.

"We confuse the success of getting a foothold with the labour of penetration. The current talk about 'Christian Presence' revives the old idea, just as if a beach-head is all that God requires."[3] In a former generation the great call was to establish bridgeheads for Christ in many previously unevangelized lands; today in many of these countries all that we have is a bridgehead. Sometimes it is a shrinking bridgehead, apparently abandoned by the army which sent out the first forces. Churchill spoke of the sick feeling he had when, in the early days of the war, he ordered Calais to be held, knowing that no relief was possible. But too many Christians today are almost heedless of such situations. We do not have even that sense of desertion that Churchill had. The churches are so often so halfhearted; missions cost money and that means less money for the building fund and the new parking lot.

Even the student Christian organizations seem to have lost the clarion call which once characterized them. In the Inter-Varsity Fellowship annual report for 1969, we are reminded that after the First World War "up to fifty per cent of the CU members went abroad as missionaries" and that again after the Second World War "a large number of members went abroad." Yes, but why not now? We need less hemming and hawing by the churches and the societies. Give us the men and we will finish the job, the Lord being our Helper. The evangelical student movements especially must not give an uncertain sound, but call as loudly and clearly today for world evangelization as they did in their earliest days.

There seems little doubt, not only from the traditional success-story biographies, but from the unwritten stories of many less-known faithful men and women, that *early attitudes and early usefulness have a lot to do in shaping those who later be-*

[3]Charles Troutman writing in *Penetracion*, occasional papers on student work in Latin America.

come mature and useful missionaries. Unfortunately not every
keen university Christian fellowship member or young people's
fellowship leader necessarily grows into a useful worker. But
the vast majority of those who are now useful workers were, in
their younger days in the services or as students in the late teens
and early twenties, already active and fruitful in the Lord's
service. It is for such people that this book is primarily intended. It is especially for those who believe that the Lord is
calling them to such work, and are willing to go if the churches
should send them, but do not know whether they are still
needed, or how they should prepare themselves, or what positive steps they should take next.

My thanks are due to the countless people who have written
other books and articles or given talks that have helped me, to
Miss Doreen Loke and Miss Eileen Gordon who typed out the
final manuscript, to my family who were prepared to let me
spend part of my vacation writing, and to my missionary brethren who have hammered out some of these issues with me.

1 The Call

TALKING FREELY in discussion with students in several countries, one meets perhaps the greatest confusion and uncertainty in thinking about what constitutes "the missionary call." This is no longer a matter for discussion only in the traditional missionary-sending countries of the West. It is equally a problem in Asia and other parts of the world where the churches recognize that all Christians have a missionary responsibility toward areas where churches have not yet been planted, as well as toward those areas where the ground is hard and growth has been slow, and where the small struggling national churches welcome the help of reinforcements from the international church.[1]

The crucial question is: How should these workers needed overseas be recruited? How will the sending churches select "internationals" to send overseas as their representatives, to plant new churches where none exists, or to work in association with emerging national churches where they do exist? In Western countries we have grown accustomed to the multiplicity of denominational and interdenominational societies, each trying to establish its claims upon our support. Are the methods adopted to make us feel responsible and to get us involved, the right ones? In order to answer such questions, the important thing is to go back to the New Testament and to check what have become traditional practices against what we find there, when the first missionaries were called and sent out by the

[1] It is suggested that as the complement of the word *nationals* the word *internationals* might be a far better word than *missionaries* if we are to eliminate the unfortunate undertones of colonialist superiority in these days when *missionaries* may be going to those who are intellectually and educationally their superiors! See pp. 33 f.

churches of Jerusalem, Antioch, and Lystra. But first of all let
us see what the current practice has been.

THE VOLUNTEER SYSTEM

The emphasis in recent years has tended to be on individuals
receiving a subjective sense of call and volunteering for full-
time Christian service. A tradition has grown up of missionary
meetings which end with an appeal to those present to offer
themselves for service overseas. Often this is carefully handled
and simply means that those who have already felt the prompt-
ings of the Lord are encouraged to make known their *willingness* to serve God overseas and thus to offer themselves, recognizing that others will then decide their *fitness*. It thus becomes a useful way for the *availability* of individuals to be recognized, without prejudice to their *suitability,* which will then
be decided by the various selection panels of Christian men and
women set up by missionary societies for that purpose.

But in some cases, unfortunately, an emotional appeal with
sentimental overtones is thrown at a group of young people
eager to do the right thing, and the result is that the more
emotional members of the audience respond. (The higher
proportion of women offering for service may be due in some
measure to this type of approach.) Experience shows, however,
that availability bears little relation to suitability, for among
such "volunteers" may be some who are a museum of patho-
logical conditions, and others who are temperamentally quite
unsuited for service in isolated parts of the world. Many of
those who were too phlegmatic, or too self-deprecating, to respond to such an appeal remain in their seats. But if a more
scriptural basis of selection were used, they too might have
responded and in the end made far better missionaries.

Some may feel that criticizing a system through which many
missionaries serving today have found their way overseas is
neither helpful nor spiritual. But God does not always prevent

us from doing things which are mistaken or unbiblical and, indeed, may overrule such actions for His glory. This does not mean, however, that we should not continually subject even long-established Christian practice to the judgment of God's Word and be prepared to reconsider our methods in the light of what we discover. In actual experience, of course, the dangers of the present system are mitigated by the selection boards and candidate committees which have had to be set up to make sure that the manifestly unsuitable volunteers are weeded out.

But this, too, raises problems which a different and more biblical method might avoid. Candidates arrive for the interview with a subjective conviction that the Lord has called them, only to find themselves turned down as unsuitable by a board. This could cause some young people to have real problems over divine guidance; they may begin questioning the leading and call of God when they should be questioning the volunteer system of men.

In my view, however, the chief practical drawback of our present system is that the candidate committees are restricted to those who actually volunteer. The need may be for differently gifted workers or more experienced ones. If volunteers with the required qualifications are not forthcoming, the committees will have to make the best possible use of those who do offer. The churches may contain many who have exactly the gifts and experience required but, if they do not volunteer, they are not available under the present system.

To meet this situation most missionary societies make a point of repeatedly stressing the kind of worker they are looking for, and encourage their supporters to pray that God will graciously lead men and women with these qualifications to them. Yet they continue to receive offers from people who are attracted to forms of missionary service which the society knows are not the most crucial and strategic at the present time. For example, in Southeast Asia today the outstanding need is for workers with evangelistic and pastoral experience who can gather together groups of converts and graft them into multiplying, growing churches. But that kind of experience and training is hard to come by in the traditional "sending" countries, because "church-planters" and "lay training experts" are not really categories that home churches—set in a more institutionalized and established mode—can produce. Thus, young people volunteering for missionary service are those whose professional qualifications can be more readily paralleled at home—nurses, doctors, accountants, secretaries, and so on. Certainly work can be found for them; but if there were a choice, the greater priority would be for those who will build congregations.

CALLING AND THE CHURCH

Apart from the practical limitations, however unsatisfactory, the volunteer system is highly suspect because it seems to have very little biblical warrant. Many of our problems in understanding the New Testament stem from our English language, where the form of the second person is the same both in the singular and in the plural. Thus the reader of the English New Testament epistles tends to understand all statements about "you" as applying personally (which is good) and individualistically (which is bad). In other languages, including the originals, it is clear that most of the injunctions are addressed to groups and congregations of Christians. Contact with Asian ways of corporate thinking lights up this aspect of New Testament teaching and throws it into violent contrast with Western individualism. Whether this arose from the American frontier spirit, the pioneer who stood on his own feet, or an every-man-for-himself mentality encouraged by Darwinism and the idea of "the survival of the fittest," is far from clear; but such attitudes are just not *Christian* at all. There must be an emphasis on teaching every man so that he will tell his neighbor and his brother, rather than putting such highly individ-

ualistic and selfish stress on subjective experience. We have
been right in stressing the need for personal experience of
Christ and a true, daily, subjective experience of fellowship
with the Lord, but wrong in our failure to develop the New
Testament doctrine of the corporate people of God.

The Greek words *klēsis* ("calling") and *ekklēsia* ("church")
are as obviously related as "establish" and "establishment," or
"proving" and "approbation." Thus when, in Ephesians 3:21,
Paul concluded his prayer for glory to God "in the church,"
he was not only following the thread of his earlier explanations
of the new corporate body transcending racial divisions, binding Gentiles and Jews together in a new nation, a new citizenry
and a new household. He follows it up naturally in 4:1 when
he "therefore" beseeches them to "live lives worthy of the call
you [plural] have received" (4:1, Williams). Because you are
members of this "summoned-out group" (like a muster, or a
posse), then behave like such people. One of my favorite defi-
nitions of the church is found in Barclay's description of the
meaning of *ekklēsia,* where he shows that the secular Greek
usage (like the Hebrew, "congregation of the people of Is-
rael") is of the summoning of the community together (as in
Ac 19:41, where the town clerk "dismissed the assembly" [*ekklēsia*] gathered in the theater at Ephesus). So the word means
a summons or call to *"every man to come and to shoulder his
responsibilities."*[2]

In New Testament thinking, then, the whole church has a
responsibility which is to be shouldered by every single member. In this sense every true Christian without exception is
"called." The Great Commission (Mt 28:19) is very commonly
expounded in an individualistic sense: "You [individual] go
and make disciples of all nations." But manifestly it must apply to every baptized and taught disciple. "You [plural] go and

[2]William Barclay, *New Testament Wordbook* (London: SCM, 1955),
p. 70.

make disciples of all nations, baptizing them [the disciples] and teaching them [every one of the disciples] to observe all that I commanded you." Every single baptized disciple is to be taught to obey every single one of Christ's commands. The command you cannot possibly overlook in this context is this very command to go and make more disciples of all nations, to baptize them, and teach them everything. The call is universal to every Christian and to be taught to every Christian. This command, then, is self-propagating. Like the man on the Quaker Oats packet who holds a packet of Quaker Oats on which is a picture of another Quaker holding another packet, with yet another picture of another Quaker holding yet another packet, with a picture of another Quaker—so it is understood that those who are called have a common responsibility to make more disciples, baptize them and teach them the responsibilities of their calling to go and make, baptize and teach more disciples. The church is thus a great world evangelization society committed to evangelism and teaching, and this *is the total responsibility of the total church*. The whole church has a missionary calling and thus the whole congregation in the New Testament is involved in "calling" missionaries.

The nearest to a volunteer system in the Bible is found in the call of Isaiah, "Whom shall I send, and who will go for us?" to which the prophet replies, "Here am I! Send me," words which find an echo in the heart of every Christian, or ought to. Yet this is not the call of a New Testament missionary, but of one Old Testament prophet, and represents a personal call of God which he heard. (We have no reason to believe it was general.) Other Old Testament heroes had a call which was quite the opposite of "volunteering": Moses did his utmost to avoid God's call; for almost two chapters he tries to wriggle out of the inescapable sovereign call of God. The calls of Nehemiah, Ezekiel, and Jeremiah are all different again. It is gratuitous to make Isaiah's call typical of all Old Testament calls, let alone of New Testament ones.

When certain men of Cyprus and Cyrene started evangelizing Greeks in Syrian Antioch, news of it came to the church in Jerusalem and the account states baldly "they *sent* Barnabas" (Ac 11:22, NASB). We are told nothing of calls for volunteers, nothing of Barnabas' own personal sense of call (we need not infer from this that he did not have one). We simply learn that the church "sent" him. The Holy Spirit, who is the Author of Scripture, singles out that point: the congregation of Christians in Jerusalem *sent* him. When you think about it, you can see the suitability of their choice.

1. He was a Cypriot Jewish Christian and therefore known to the Antioch evangelists (Ac 11:20), many of whom were Cypriots.

2. He was a good man and full of the Holy Spirit (Ac 11:24).

3. While his name was Joseph, his nickname Barnabas, meaning "Son of Encouragement" (Ac 4:36, NASB), indicates an aspect of his character seen already in his earlier appearances in the Acts narrative. This is actually alluded to in Acts 11 where "he *encouraged* [*parakaleō*] them all" (v. 23). In the Western text of verse 26 it reads that Barnabas *encouraged* (*parakaleō*) Saul to come back to Antioch.

Barnabas appears to have been chosen for his suitable qualities and sent by the church as the best man they had available for the task.

Saul got to Antioch also, not because of a subjective, individualistic call, but because Barnabas went to "look for him" (the word implies difficulty in discovering his whereabouts in Tarsus) and *"brought* him" to Antioch (Ac 11:26). In spite of Paul's very clear call on the Damascus road thirteen years earlier, it was the initiative of another which brought him to Antioch.

When, a year later, Barnabas and Saul set out on the first missionary journey, it was no individualistic decision. Acts 13: 1-3 makes it clear that the Lord spoke to the whole group of leaders in the Antioch church, including the two men who were sent. It was a group decision.

Later Paul and Barnabas have a hot argument[3] and part company. Paul *chooses* Silas (Ac 15:40), previously elected and sent by the church of Jerusalem to carry its decrees to the churches of the Gentiles in Antioch, Syria, and Cilicia. He was a leading man among the brethren (Ac 15:22), a prophet himself (15:32), and thus qualified to accompany Paul on his mission.

On return to Galatia they meet Timothy, "well spoken of by the brethren in Lystra and Iconium" (Ac 16:2, NASB) and *Paul wanted to take him.* Again we are not told what Timothy thought or felt at being wrested from the apron strings of Lois and Eunice, but the Holy Spirit tells us that the initiative was taken by Paul.

In all the four instances, then, of sending out Barnabas, Saul, Silas, and Timothy, what the New Testament emphasizes is *not* the initiative of the individual, nor his own subjective sense of call, *but always* the initiative of others, either of a congregation or of other Christians already active in such work.

SUBJECTIVE CALL, OBJECTIVELY CONFIRMED

Please do not misunderstand me. We have tended traditionally to stress the personal and subjective nature of the call of God to full-time service. I would not want to remove any of that stress. A man needs to be sure that God has called him. He needs an inner conviction that it is not a personal whim, a subjective delusion, nor mere emotional excitement that has

[3]The archaic "the contention was sharp" of the KJV should not be allowed to obscure the fact that two men "filled with the Spirit" were not impeccable, and should prevent us from espousing any doctrine of sinless perfection as a result of spiritual experience.

put him into the ministry at home or abroad, but the call of
God Himself. When there is opposition, difficulty, temptation,
doubt, depression, or disappointment, a person needs to be certain that he has really been called of God.

But how is the individual to be sure he is not deceiving himself? That he does not rather imagine himself in a surplice,
six feet above contradiction in a pulpit, able to hold captive
an unwilling congregation who has to listen to him? That
he has not been carried away by the well-written missionary
biography and is attracted by the lure of the tribal hills or the
glamour of the Himalayas? Some sterling souls are definite
and certain about everything, even when to other people they
seem to be manifestly misguided and wrong. But others need
objective confirmation of their own genuine subjective sense
of call. This is found, I would suggest, in the New Testament
pattern, in the objective recognition of that call, *first,* by the
congregation, or by the group of Christians who know that individual best: they know his gifts and usefulness. It may also
be confirmed, *second,* by the invitation of those involved already in some distant work of evangelism and church-planting, who, on the recommendation of the church, see here a
potential fellow worker. Thus together with the subjective
sense of the call of God ("I feel the Lord wants me") , there is
the objective confirmation of the sending church ("We feel
the Lord wants you to go and wants us to send you") , and of
the receiving mission (ary) ("We know that there is a need and,
from all we hear of you, we believe that you are the kind of
person that the Lord wants to be with us") .

INDIVIDUAL CALL, CORPORATELY CONFIRMED

You will have already felt the contrast, I am sure, between
the present existing situation in most churches and the New
Testament pattern of missionary sending. Many congregations
have little sense of direct responsibility for those "miserable

enthusiasts"[4] who feel called. Ironically, our individualization
of missions has been accompanied also by a depersonalization,
so that churches have quotas and budgets which are given to a
denominational or interdenominational society traditionally
supported. It is hard to feel much enthusiasm for giving or
praying for a set of initials, however widely esteemed. Elsewhere one meets the extraordinary phenomenon of a church
speaking of "our missionary" and yet being content to send
him $150 a year without inquiring too closely just how much
it really costs to support him and his family.[5]

Missionary societies are partly to blame. They have been
prepared too often to accept candidates without more than a
nod to the local church from which he comes. They may ask,
perhaps, for recommendation papers from the minister, but
make little or no attempt to involve the whole congregation
and its leadership. But if a church, a congregation, have together prayed and sought the will of God to know which of
their gifted young couples, which leader of their youth work
or men's group, they should send, then two people intimately
known to them—George and Margaret—have gone out. They
will pray not for unknown persons but for two friends who are
facing difficulties now, because they sent them where they are
and are thus very responsible to pray for them. Moreover, if
they send them, they will not be happy to let them starve and
go without. They are *ours,* an expression of the corporate missionary activity of the whole congregation.

FACING THINGS AS THEY ARE

Let's be realistic. I have tried to set out what I believe is the
New Testament pattern for sending out missionaries and of
the call to full-time service, whether at home or abroad. It is

[4]According to Morris of Clipstone, Dr. Ryland told William Carey that
he was a "miserable enthusiast" when he posed his question about the
church's use of means for reaching the heathen.
[5]See chap. 5.

a corporate and fully church-centered approach. But today many of us have to face very different situations and may belong to congregations which are frankly uninterested in missions and have little corporate church life of any depth at all. Again, because of the peripatetic nature of student life (and this holds for nurses and many other professionals who move away from their home churches for training, or who are converted during training and so scarcely have a home church at all), students may attend congregations in their place of work or in the town where they are studying and are welcomed as visitors, but are often not properly integrated into the church at all. Or, all too rarely, there are situations where churches already have more missionaries than they can support and they cannot take on every member of the local university, college, or hospital Christian fellowship who attends their services and who is considering Christian work overseas. There are other situations where all the church effort goes into supporting a denominational work, sometimes one that does not enjoy our full confidence regarding its doctrinal stand. Or, more commonly, even in churches which are thoroughly evangelical, once a year a representative of some missionary group speaks at a missionary weekend for half an hour, more or less, about the work and very often all is forgotten within the next few days. So you reply: "I like your ideal, and wish we had it; but what do I do in the existing situation? If I wait for my church to send me I shall never go."

In reply I would urge first of all that we should work toward and pray toward a greater realization of that New Testament corporate responsibility for evangelization both at home and abroad which I have tried to suggest. Obviously those who become ministers of home churches have the greatest responsibility and the greatest opportunity by their direct teaching and enthusiastic leadership to reform churches in this direction. In one sense this corporate approach to sending missionaries is only one by-product of reforming the church, so that it again becomes what it was meant to be. For too long we have been content with superficiality, with institutionalism, and a formal, meeting-centered church.

But many churches, unfortunately, are led by those who do not see the point of missionary work at all and concentrate their concern on other aspects of the church's activity. As far as finance is concerned, they may be genuinely fearful lest missionary interest should become too dominant and divert to itself funds and personnel which they feel must be retained for use at home. Under such circumstances what should those persons do who have a sense of the call of God now? They cannot wait for the reformation of the church at home. In some parts of the world the first bridgehead still has to be established. In others the force is small, ill-supported, and making little progress. Elsewhere the churches need reform and revival every bit as much as the churches in our homeland.

In practical terms and on the local level something might well be done with the young people in the church, our own contemporaries. A cell group for prayer is not so hard to start. If we do not have the initiative to begin such a group, we probably lack certain essential missionary qualities anyway. Such a young people's group might well later pray and give to support some of their number as missionaries. And if through such a group a more corporate approach to missionary endeavor is achieved, this could become a source of great blessing to the whole congregation, leading to that deeper church fellowship for which so many are longing. The life of the local church will be one of the missionary's leading concerns overseas. So now is a good time to start preparing by seeking to encourage such an attitude in our own home churches.

As regards personal preparation, there is, of course, much that can be done; it is with this aspect that this book is chiefly concerned. Here is a brief checklist:

Examine the needs. What kinds of missionaries are most needed, and in what places? What am I most interested in and most suited for? There are openings for people with highly sophisticated and specialized training. But if all were like this we might lack workers for the main job that needs to be done: making disciples, baptizing them, and teaching them (see chap. 2).

Examine your qualities. Do you have what it takes physically and emotionally? Clearly those with physical or nervous deficiencies must be excluded. But what about experience and usefulness in the Lord's work already? If you are already active in Christian work, this indicates that you possibly have the essential qualities (see chap. 4).

Endeavor to gain qualifications. Not only academic or professional qualifications are needed, which might gain you an entrance into some overseas country, but also theological and Bible training to make you a qualified evangelist and competent teacher of the Word of God (see chap. 3).

Establish some links with various missionary societies. You do not commit yourself by reading their literature, taking their magazines and reading them prayerfully, and joining together with other like-minded people to pray for the work. But through access to such information, your sense of call and concern will be deepened and accurately informed. Societies will not just send out anyone by the next plane, but they will tell you what kind of missionaries they need, and where and what training they would advise. But we deal more in detail later with each of these things.

Perhaps it would be good to close this section on corporate calling and responsibility by reminding ourselves of William Carey's words to his friend Andrew Fuller: "Will we separate again, and do nothing?" The stress is on "we." As we look to the future, we shall always want to go as representatives of a congregation, with others standing behind us who will pray for us, and be intimately involved with us, although geographically remote. Therefore it is good to involve others in prayer with us, that we may freely talk about the future and share God's guidance with one another. If young people's groups and fellowships saw more of such corporate concern for the use we make of our "just one life," how wonderful that would be!

2 The Need

IT IS GOOD that most things are questioned these days, and the question of whether missionaries are still necessary and whether they are still needed is an important one. Are white missionaries really "white elephants" today? In this chapter I want to try to deal briefly with various objections and queries. Some question the need on humanistic grounds ("Surely people are all right as they are, with their own religions, and don't have to be converted to Christianity") or on anthropological grounds ("Missionaries interfere with cultures"). Others have the idea that, now that national churches have taken over in most places, missionaries are a kind of expensive ecclesiological anachronism. Thus in this chapter I want to establish first of all that full-time Christian workers are still needed both at home and abroad, and then to try to show what kinds and categories of worker are most required.

PROSELYTIZING FROM OTHER RELIGIONS

To speak today of the "heathen" seems as ill-mannered as to talk of "backward countries." That some countries are less prosperous than others is obvious, but this is perhaps because they have been exploited by the more developed countries, and so we charitably speak of "underdeveloped" or "developing" countries, feeling our own guilt if we belong to the countries which are former colonial powers. In these days when educated leaders meet at the United Nations and innumerable international conferences, the whole attitude of regarding people as "heathen in their blindness" seems altogether inappropriate.

Humanistic and relativistic attitudes to truth are so com-

monplace in our educational systems that even Christians may
hold views which are really inconsistent with their supposed
doctrinal convictions. In separate compartments they seem to
believe concurrently that no views are necessarily completely
wrong, and that all points of view are equally valid and ought
to be respected; *and* that the human mind is fallible and cor-
rupted, and needs to be recalibrated in terms of the categories
that God has revealed to us. Thus even some professing Christians may be in doubt about the validity of converting men of
other "faiths," suggesting as it does a kind of intellectual in-
tolerance out of joint with the spirit of our age.

This question may be answered both biblically and pragmatically. It is not difficult to discover the biblical estimate
of "religions":

1. In the Old Testament other religions are anathema to
the one true God; their idols are to be utterly destroyed, and
intermarriage with idolaters is forbidden. Idol worship is
foolish and wicked.

2. Religions are human superstitions, the result of misguided human imagination, speculation, and deliberate re-
bellion against God (Ro 1:23).

3. There are nonetheless evil and demonic powers behind
superstitious religion: "What pagans sacrifice they offer to
demons and not to God" (1 Co 10:20, RSV).

4. The Christian way of salvation is the only way. It is
sometimes argued that God may well have spoken to men
through other religions as well as through Jesus Christ, and
that we ought to give them the benefit of the doubt; they may
be mere human superstitions, yet God might have spoken
through them. The Bible does not deny that God has spoken
to men outside Christianity and, for example, Christians fully
accept the Jewish Scriptures as authoritative and inspired by
the same Lord in whom both Jews and Christians believe. Yet,
what is the attitude of Jesus Christ and the apostles to Judaism?

It is Jews whom Peter insists must "repent, and be baptized
. . . in the name of Jesus" (Ac 2:38 ff.), and to whom he
insists: "There is salvation in no one else; for there is no other
name under heaven that has been given among men, by which
we must be saved" (4:12, NASB). Paul, the converted Jewish
zealot, has the same view. In his sample sermon in the syna-
gogue at Pisidian Antioch, he tells them that, in the gospel,
they may be "freed from all things, from which you could not
be freed through the law of Moses" (see Ac 13:38 ff., NASB).
It is notable that Christ tells the most devout leaders of the
Jews that only by trust in Him is there salvation for Jews, for
otherwise they will die in their sins. Thus, even with regard
to this "great world religion" about which there can be no
doubt that it stems from a true revelation from the true Lord
God, Christians are unequivocal in insisting that conversion to
Christ is necessary. Good and excellent though the Jewish precepts are, they cannot save.

5. Neither intellectual excellence nor philosophical wisdom
is able to save men. This can be demonstrated from the attitude of the apostles to the educated Greeks. Greece had produced many great and respected thinkers—Plato, Socrates,
Aristotle. But this had not kept them from idolatry, and
though God had "winked at" the times of their ignorance,
"He now commands all men everywhere to repent" (Ac 17:30,
Williams).[1]

Biblically, then, it is clear that the very universality of the
Christian claim, based upon a unique revelation through the
incarnate Christ and a unique work of atonement on the cross,
demands an entirely exclusive claim.

Pragmatically, there are questions to be asked. Is it really
true that people living in Muslim or Buddhist countries are
"all right as they are" and happy in their beliefs? Do all religions actually lead men to God?

[1]Paul preaching in Athens.

1. Not all religions even try; Confucius was himself agnostic about God.

2. It all depends on what is meant by God. Buddhism does not try to lead men to God in a Christian sense at all. Human consciousness is an illusion of reality, and man is just a transient image reflected in the surface of impersonal totality. This is a world of dew, and the sensations reaching us through our sense organs have no objective reference; it is all a dream. But such a view of life does not satisfy the common desire of men for reality. When the one surviving child of the Japanese poet Issa died, his friends came to comfort him. They told him that this is an unreal, transient world of dew, and that he should remind himself that neither he nor his child had any objective reality. So he wrote: *"Tsuyu no yo wa, tsuyu no yo nagara, sarinagara . . ."* ("A world of dew is a world of dew, and yet . . . and yet . . .").

It is no comfort to know that those we have known are mere illusions, in the mind of a pantheistic total reality.

3. The actual beliefs of the people are unrelated to the pure essence of their religion, as expounded in the academic context. Buddhist priests in Japan ought to spend their lives in pursuit of enlightenment. In practice, the priests spend much of their time reciting the *sutras* (in Sanskrit or medieval Chinese, and quite incomprehensible to the modern Japanese) to the spirit of the recently deceased to prevent their interfering with the living. In other words, they are motivated by an animistic fear of the dead. Similar beliefs underlie Buddhism in other parts of Southeast Asia. It is just not true that "people are happy as they are"; the bulk of them are bewildered and lost in superstitious darkness and fear of death.

4. Even when a religion tries to bring a man to God, does it succeed? I remember once a delightful Muslim student replying indignantly, "We have salvation in Islam: six circles of hell, and paradise." I grinned at him and asked, "And to

which of them are you going?" The warm brown eyes looked puzzled. "I do not know," he said.

A SOCIOLOGICAL JUSTIFICATION

How can you justify interfering with tribal cultures? Few people these days still hold to the fiction of the happy primeval savage, splendid and unspoiled. Nevertheless it is widely felt that Christian missionaries, if they are successful, must change, and therefore spoil, local cultures. How can one justify such an intrusion? To this I would reply as follows:

1. Cultures are not static things but are in a constant state of change. This is especially true today. In Thailand the desire is to ensure that all should learn the Thai language and be assimilated to its culture, whether they are immigrant Chinese shopkeepers in the cities, one of the million Malay-speaking Muslims in the south, or belong to the ethnic minority groups (Lisu, Meo tribes, etc.) in the northern mountains. The effect of urbanization, the impact of mass communications, the educational explosion—all these are bound to affect cultures; they are changing anywhere and everywhere, quite apart from the effect of a handful of missionaries.

2. By learning the language of a tribal group and committing it to writing, and by a study of tribal culture and thought, missionaries have actually done a good deal to preserve tribal cultures which might otherwise have just disappeared.

3. Some cultures or aspects of cultures need to be changed. In one North Thailand group, for example, most of the children are today bought from other tribes. Women do not seem to have more than one or two children of their own, and these are usually born to them in their teens and before they are married. This suggests infertility due to venereal disease resulting from the very free sexual relations between teenagers. In former days this was frowned on and severely punished,

and women had large families of their own; but sexual promiscuity seems to have led to the present sad situation of infertility. The introduction of a Christian code of sexual conduct in the churches should see the restoration of the previous
happy ability to bear their own children.

A great deal more could be said on this subject. It cannot
be denied that terrible mistakes have been made and that some
earnest Christians seem to have been insensitive to cultural
differences in thinking, and have failed to distinguish between
what is merely a cultural irrelevance of Western Christendom
and what is essentially Christian and biblical. The greatest
cruelties have been done in compelling converted polygamists
to dismiss additional wives, thus condemning these unfortunate women to lives of poverty or even of prostitution.

Again, it seems tragic that pseudo-Gothic architecture and
cassocks and surplices should be regarded as worthy of export
as though they were integral to essential Christian worship.
It is depressing to have to sing poor translations of not very
inspiring English hymns set to the same old Western tunes
when a national culture can produce its own spontaneous
praise. In Thailand the most appreciated hymns are pentatonic, as is the indigenous music. There are many ways in
which the national and local cultures may adorn the worship
and life of the churches, without in any way involving compromise with that which is unbiblical or a syncretism with
pagan beliefs and idolatrous customs.

Isn't Missionary Work Finished?

Many of us have seen pictures of flourishing churches, with
their own national pastors. We see bishops of many nationalities attending Lambeth Conference and other international
conferences. We meet very fine men from overseas training in
our theological colleges. How does this tie in with the continuing need for missionaries? Yesterday I saw two missionary

magazines, one from Africa and one from South America, both appealing for more workers to join them. Is it just missionaries who feel that they need reinforcements? Is not the time coming when they will not be needed anymore? None of us wants to embark upon a lifework which is found to be redundant before we have really started.

Take this quotation, for example:

> I am less sanguine than many others, but it is my confident belief that if the missionary societies are faithful to their charge . . . you need not after [next year] . . . send any more missionaries to Japan. You will need to support the men already there and the institutions for a while, but no new men will need to go. The finishing up of the work can be safely left to the foreign force which will by that time be there, working in conjunction with the ever increasing number of native pastors and evangelists.

So wrote the missionary Guido Verbeck in 1889 (the unfashionable word "native" gives it away).[2] In the year he wrote, the church was growing very rapidly, and many really expected that Japan would be a Christian country by the end of the nineteenth century. At any rate, there was a strong reaction in 1890 against everything foreign; the church was persecuted by militarists from without and weakened by "modernists" from within, and even today less than 1 percent of Japanese are professing Christians.

When I was in theological college we often prayed for a former student who had become a bishop in his native country. I might have imagined that there was a flourishing church in that country, had I not recently talked with an Operation Mobilization worker who was there and discovered that there are less than 2,000 professing Christians in the whole country!

The quotation in the introduction from Charles Troutman is worth repeating here: "We confuse the success of getting a foothold with the labour of penetration . . . just as if a beach-

[2]Quoted in Augustus Pieters, *Mission Problems in Japan* (1912).

head is all that God requires." We must not be misled because
we hear that in some part of Africa there is a fully organized,
self-governing, self-supporting church and that no more Christian workers from outside are needed. This would not even be
true of all parts of Africa, let alone of other parts of the world.
Each national (and local) situation is different. Korea has
one Christian in every fourteen people but Thailand has only
one in 1,000. Indonesia is made up of many quite distinct
ethnic groups with their own languages; some have strong
churches (up to 40 percent of a population may be Christian),
others are in rapid growth, some yet totally unevangelized.
Thus we may distinguish between:

1. *Pioneer-phase countries* with a tiny emerging church, or
perhaps without any Christian witness. The main task of
evangelism lies ahead. The need for missionaries is so obvious
that we need not elaborate.

2. *Patchwork-phase countries* where the church exists, but
where it has failed to reach certain geographical areas (e.g.,
Indonesia), ethnic groups (e.g., Malaysia), social strata (e.g.,
Laos) or rural areas (e.g., Japan). Thus the ethnic minorities,
the tribal hill people, have been neglected by the main national churches in Thailand and the Philippines. In many
Western countries the church is a middle-class church and
there is a sad failure to reach the working classes. A self-
governing and self-supporting church may exist, and yet it may
not be self-propagating. Many old churches have been self-
governing for centuries, but ceased propagating years ago.
Again in such patchwork-phase countries, international Christians may be needed to work alongside national Christians in
reaching the unreached areas. This group would represent the
most typical picture today.

3. *Penetrated-phase countries* where a strong church is established over most of the country and throughout most of

society (e.g., Korea). Such countries are extremely rare, unfortunately.

4. *Recession-phase countries.* The national church, once planted, has become devotionally cold, spiritually dead, or even theologically apostate. The church has gone into recession, and the younger generation still needs to be reached and evangelized. A great deal of Europe and North America is in this state, and maybe international missionaries from Africa and Asia will need to come to the rescue of the struggling national churches here! What I want to make plain is that there is no "terminal phase" reached, short of the Lord's return. In the early centuries, Asia Minor and North Africa were Christian strongholds; today both areas need to be evangelized. China once had a growing national church. Today that church no longer exists as an organized body.

On a short-term view of (Anglo-Saxon) missions since William Carey, it could be thought that world evangelization began again at that time; that, in the 150 years since then, country after country has been entered and churches planted; that now more and more are reaching a "terminal phase" and all the missionaries can go home. This *is* a very short-term view, often associated with the "closing doors" syndrome that gets some people so worried. When Carey started, all the doors were closed, including British India; he got in by living in the Danish colony of Serampore. Henry Martyn got in as a British army chaplain. Adoniram Judson could not get into India at all and went to Burma. It is true that in recent years some countries have closed and others seem to be closing to foreign missionaries of the conventional type, but it is also true that other doors have opened. When doors close they often slam shut with a loud noise; when they open, they do it quietly with a minimum of publicity.

Evangelization is not a stationary, once-for-all task; it must be repeated in every generation in every country.

MISSIONS AND THE NATIONAL CHURCH

Listening to some theorists ("missiologist" is the horrid current word), one has the impression that we are committed to a mission-of-the-gaps theology,[3] a steadily shrinking role in which missions do only those things which national churches cannot do for themselves. This means that, on this theory, missions require a steadily shrinking force of steadily increasing specialization and sophistication, until theological professors, mass communications experts, and purveyors of the latest gimmickry on world promotion tours will be the only international contribution to fully fledged national churches!

The alternative is to believe that there will always be some international involvement in every land. It seems strange to adopt a missionary-go-home policy in which we have increasingly nationalistic churches, and then suddenly the final whistle blows, the last trump is sounded and, presto! we have an international church in heaven. It seems more in accord with our expectation of that great multitude which no man can number, from every tribe, tongue, and nation, to believe that also *on earth* God's will may be done, and that we shall see a steady growth of the international aspect of the church until the day of consummation comes.

As for closing doors, Christ told His disciples that when they were persecuted in one city, they were to flee to another (Mt 10:23).[4] There always have been closing doors and opening ones. Probably there always will be. On the long-term view, world evangelization is being continually interrupted by wars, revolutions, and political difficulties. The history of Christian work in China is an outstanding example of this.

The churches cannot afford to go in for nationalistic isolation, any more than nations can. We desperately need one

---

[3]Just as in a "God-of-the-gaps" theology, God is only a hypothesis drawn in to explain things for which current science has no other explanation, thus creating a steadily shrinking role.
[4]See pp. 128 ff.

another in the international church. In the last decade it is estimated that the number of young people under twenty in Asia and the Far East (excluding communist countries) increased by 175 million.[5] In the "open" countries of East Asia we estimate an increase of the population from 372 to 478 million in the next ten years. At present, the small national churches are already failing to reach the existing population effectively and, facing an extra 100 million in ten years, they badly need reinforcement from the international church.

"Missions" is the method by which the churches of the world are always mobilizing their most effective workers and sending them to the pioneer areas and the problem spots of the world. They are both the growth hormones and the white corpuscles, as it were, of the Christian body. Let me quote an Indian Christian on the subject:

> There is no place for national isolation in the Christian church. The mission of the church is not the job of any one national church. There is enough need to challenge the churches from all nations. Another important point is that the Christian church, whether in Asia or elsewhere, cannot give up its character as a body transcending racial and national barriers. It is supranational and should never be bound by a narrow nationalism. . . . This must be expressed especially in countries where there are increasing restrictions upon the entry of foreign missionaries and the church is pressurised to be purely a national institution. . . . There is no place for the feeling that the foreign missionary should be here as long as he is needed and then pull out when he has performed his task. In the supranational fellowship of the church which has a worldwide mission, the foreign missionary need not be a temporary factor.[6]

THE NEED FOR A NEW MISSIONARY ATTITUDE

Missionaries are thus still needed, not only to go from West-

[5]Quoted from an ECAFE report (Economic Council for Asia and the Far East).

[6]Theodore Williams in a paper on "The Asian Churches and their Mission" at the Singapore Congress on Evangelism.

ern countries to *Africasia* (Dr. Donald MacGavran's useful
word for Africa, South America and Asia) , but from all continents to all continents. I am assuming that Caucasian-
dominated missions are doomed to extinction. The image of
the word *missionary* has not always been good, especially when
someone has had an ax to grind and blamed the missionary for
world troubles, or made him an object of ridicule or scorn.
One winces at D. T. Niles' description of the missionary as "a
representative of the foreignness of the Gospel in any human
situation." It may be better to drop the word, especially when
used in opposition to *national,* which in its turn was a replace-
ment for the old word *native,* though that was a perfectly good
word when properly used of an autochthonous inhabitant!
The word *internationals* may be a good alternative, especially
as it stresses the need for missionaries to be drawn from all
races and all national churches. White missionaries are not
"white elephants," provided they will work in a team as equals
with missionaries from Africa and Asia. We rejoice at the increasing missionary concern and involvement of churches in
India, Japan, Korea, the Philippines, and other Asian countries.

While the theorists and the missiologists argue in their
learned journals, the missionary on the ground at grips with
the enemy is in no doubt that reinforcements are needed. From
almost everywhere comes the call for "more workers." These
are not just posts cooked up by missions following Parkinson's
rule. Again and again we receive *invitations from national
churches themselves:* Please send us a missionary to help in
an outreach from such-and-such a church; to help at this university or college.

All over the world the greatest need is for "church-starters."
The growth of population is such that an apparent growth
rate of (say) 10 percent in the church may represent only a

biological increase in Christian families, and none being won from "paganism."

Nobody wants useless missionaries—mere ecumenical symbols, ciphers acting as liaison officers, and sources of foreign money. But there is one kind of missionary that everyone wants. That is the person who will identify himself closely with the people to whom he goes, ready to accept the living standards, to follow the customs and use the thought patterns of the country to which he goes, using them to lead men and women to Christ, and helping in planting new congregations in the mushrooming cities and the scattered villages alike. Missionaries who are soul-winners and church-starters are never likely to be outdated. They are welcome in any country, welcome in our own, welcome everywhere.

* * *

Dear Lord, when I see the needs, I want to become the kind of person who can be used to meet them. Lord, shape my life and use me for Your glory now, and show me where I should go to tell men about You. Amen.

3   Qualifications: What Is Needed

WE HAVE TO ASK: What for? What is the primary aim of full-time Christian work? Surely it is concerned with making converts and establishing congregations. There is a real problem here in that, in the older missionary-sending countries, most churches and congregations have been in existence for many years. These are unfortunately very few people, therefore, who have had the experience of pioneering a new congregation. To some the very idea of starting a new congregation might even seem schismatic. We are often so conditioned by our background that the content which we give to the idea of "a church" is static, institutional, and building-centered. To those who have grown up in such situations, a missionary situation is hard to visualize.

The great need is for people who can go into a city of several tens of thousands where there is no church at all and where no one has ever seen a Christian home. The missionary must start from scratch, leading people to Christ, and then gathering them together into a viable, growing fellowship which he instructs until it can produce its own leaders and teachers. Alternatively, a similar work may need to be done in a large number of villages scattered across an agricultural plain, or on the fast-growing edges of some vast and rapidly expanding Asian city.[1]

[1]Total Asian population   1920: 1023×10^6
                                            1960: 1652×10^6 (61 percent increase)

      Urban population (20,000 plus)   1920: 66×10^6
                                            1960: 276×10^6 (318 percent increase)

      Primate cities (over 50,000)   Increase from 1920 to 1960: 640 percent

These figures show the importance of planting new congregations in urban areas.

The popular but vague "every Christian is a missionary" attitude, while it may say something about witness, is just not true in terms of the gifts and abilities required to start a new cell group, Bible study group, or congregation from scratch. Would, of course, that it were true, but the fact is that there is a great shortage of missionaries of this kind. As was mentioned earlier, people volunteer to be doctors, nurses, accountants and secretaries because such professions exist in the homelands. The profession of "church-planter" or "lay trainer" does not exist as such in most sending countries.

MISSIONARIES AND APOSTLES

The word *missionary* is derived from the Latin equivalent of the Greek word *apostolos,* from which we derive the word *apostle;* both words mean "one who is sent." As we have seen already, the New Testament missionary does not appear to have been a volunteer, but one who, like Barnabas, was "sent" by the church. Alan Stibbs writes:

> Though we usually think of an apostle as one of "the twelve", in the New Testament the word "apostle" is also sometimes used to describe evangelists of the pioneer sort: that is, workers sent by the Lord to preach the gospel to those who had not before heard it; and such men were sometimes used of God to found new local churches of Christian believers. For instance Barnabas and Paul, who at the call of God were separated and ordained by the church in Antioch, and sent forth by the Holy Ghost to preach the gospel in Cyprus and South Galatia, are in the course of the subsequent record of their work described as "apostles" (Acts 14:14). Later, in writing to the Christians at Thessalonica, St. Paul similarly refers to Silas, Timothy and himself as "apostles of Christ" (I Thessalonians 2:6). The word we should use nowadays is "missionaries".[2]

Great care is needed here because the "apostles of the Lord"

[2]A. M. Stibbs, *Christian Ministry* (London: Church Pastoral-Aid Soc., Falcon Books, 1960), p. 7.

were a unique group of those who had been with Christ from the start of His ministry and were witnesses of His resurrection. As such, they were specially commissioned and inspired by the Holy Spirit for the recording of Scripture and, in view of this definition, no other men could succeed them as apostles. While we must agree that the "apostles of the churches," such as Barnabas, Silas, Timothy, and other unnamed persons, were not on a par with the "apostles of the Lord," this wider usage of the word should be recognized as the equivalent of the modern word *missionary*.

In Ephesians we are given a list of, first, the itinerant ministers—the apostles, prophets, and evangelists, that is, the peripatetic travelers with a wider ministry—and then we have the settled ministers of the local congregations, the pastors and teachers. The whole passage is a striking one because of its vivid imagery taken from Psalm 68:18, which seems to describe David's capture of the Jebusite stronghold which became the city of Jerusalem (see Eph 4:8). In such a capture, plunder and booty are to be given to the victorious followers, not only of goods but also of human beings taken captive and given as slaves by the victor to his people. In the same way the victorious Christ gives gifts to His church, bondslaves (v. 11) who are, respectively, apostles, prophets, evangelists and, locally, pastors and teachers. This is interesting in these days of discussion about the status of the ministry. Far from being a heirarchy of rulers, they are the slaves of the people of God, presented to them by Christ. It is in this context that Paul sees himself as such a trophy, "a prisoner for the Lord" (v. 1).

It is also true that the pioneer missionary (especially when he goes to a people who are illiterate and who have none of the Scriptures in their own language) is uniquely an apostle who brings to them the Word of God. When the Scriptures are translated they may read them for themselves, but until then the human vessel has all the responsibility for passing on the authentic Christian gospel. Thus in such phrases as "George Hunter—Apostle of Turkestan" we give some recognition to this lesser, but nonetheless honored, apostolate. The founder of such a church often enjoys, in a peculiar sense, an authority which he cannot pass on to any successor, because he first brought to them the gospel. Paul uses the word in this sense, I believe, when he argues, "If to others I am not an apostle, at least I am to you" (1 Co 9:2, NASB), because he had been the first to bring the gospel to them.

What Is a Missionary?

In this highly technical sense, then, not all members of missionary societies are missionaries in that sense of apostleship. The Christian doctor or teacher working in a secular institution may play as full or even a fuller part than someone with similar training working in a mission hospital or school. There seems little reason to call one and not the other a missionary merely because one is supported through a missionary society and the other is not. I am not suggesting for a moment that such work, either inside or outside a missionary society, is of inferior value to the other; both play an equally important part in making a general witness to the love of Christ and the concern of Christians. Those working in both secular and mission-related institutions may play a considerable part in breaking down prejudice in resistant areas, and in direct evangelism in the conversion of patients, national staff, pupils and colleagues.

But while this is all part of the witness of the church, it is not the reason for the existence of missionary societies in the proper sense. The essential work of missionaries is "the saving of souls, the baptism of bodies, and the multiplying of churches," according to Dr. MacGavran. The aim is always to establish new self-propagating congregations in places where such did not exist before. Even in countries where an organ-

ized group of churches, either in a loose affiliation or a more
tightly knit Presbyterian or Episcopalian structure, already exists, the need to plant more churches nearly always continues.
Today the greatest challenge is afforded by the detribalized and
depersonalized growing areas, the great urban conglomerations,
the megapolis areas of the world. The great need in such countries is for missionaries who will take up residence in slums or
in high-rise apartments and start cell groups and new congregations. And even in less urbanized societies, the unreached
peasant communities and the coastal fishing villages continue
to present a challenge. When Augustus Pieters wrote in 1912
about the coastal fishing villages of Japan, he wondered when
they would be evangelized. We still wonder.

Thus what I want to stress above everything else in this book
is the need for missionaries who will dedicate themselves to
this basic task. There are other "auxiliary" ministries (sometimes termed "specialist," but this is misleading if people therefore think they are superior or more significant—they may not
be), but what matters is the planting, establishing, and teaching of the churches. All "specialist" work is only auxiliary to
this, and its usefulness should be measured in terms of the
degree to which it helps the growth of the churches.

Experience shows that it is hard to establish a Bible school
or seminary *until* there are churches which can produce promising men to be trained, and to support such workers after they
have been trained. University student work (and I speak with
a sense of deep personal involvement) can also be critical in
breaking open resistant intellectual classes, and in producing
more highly educated leaders for the churches. But again and
again student work founders because there are no local evangelical churches in which its members may be built up, and
in which they may pass on from the more temporary student
Christian fellowship stage to a fully orbed local church life.
Continually the problem is that young graduates feel at a loss,

because there are no local churches to which they may become attached and where they may be fed from the Word of God. Literature ministries, radio ministries and the like, crucial though they are in getting the gospel out, and fruitful though they are in producing individual converts, are yet frustrated again and again where there are no live congregations to follow them up and give new converts a warm welcome into Christian fellowship.

The job that most needs doing nearly everywhere, then, is *starting new congregations*. This is obviously true in pioneer and patchwork areas. The mushrooming cities are a special challenge.

TRAINING FOR CHURCH-PLANTING

It follows that the most necessary qualifications and training are for such work. But where may such people be found, and how can they be trained? Missions ask for "church-planters" or for "lay training experts"—and get no response. Doctors, nurses, teachers and so forth, secretaries, accountants: all of these there are, but not the key people! Are we asking for the moon? Do such people exist? They do. Some of them will be those with ministerial experience at home, especially in new housing areas, or in some other pioneer venture. Others will have been workers who have pioneered as traveling secretaries of various evangelical societies (usually a lot of training is involved there). Others will have been involved in starting new house churches, cell groups, or student Christian groups. It is more the quality of being a soul-winner and a group-gatherer which we should look out for. It is this determination to break fresh ground and to adopt Christian approaches to a rapidly changing situation which is needed.

When Aquila and Priscilla had a church which met in their house, where they also plied their trade as tentmakers, the same building served the triple purpose of home, workshop, and church meeting place. There seems to be more scriptural warrant for meeting in homes and workshops than in special church buildings, convenient though they may be. In the Middle Ages the system of manors and villages lent itself to the parish church concept. The parish system is a remnant of the old Piers Plowman ecclesiology. You may still see it not only in rural Europe, but in the countryside of Korea or North Sumatra: a church building surrounded by the villagers' houses.

The Industrial Revolution and subsequent urbanization has changed all this, however; Aquila now goes by bus and train, commuting to the large tentmaking factory on the other side of the city. Meetings centered in the church near their home tend to draw women rather than men, for Priscilla stays at home and gets to know her neighbors. But Aquila is more than embarrassed when asked to bring his neighbors to the guest service or gospel meeting on Sunday night; the people he knows best, his fellow workers, live on the other side of the city. Worship should be centered in the regular meeting place, but it seems doubtful if effective evangelism *can* be. In Asian urban areas, Priscilla and other wives go out to work as well, so only the grandmas, who tend to be the custodians of the old religions anyway, are at home minding the children. Such situations demand people who can develop new ways and approaches. Television makes it even less likely that Aquila will know many of his neighbors—but that is another story.[3]

THEOLOGICAL AND BIBLE TRAINING

It is sometimes overlooked that half the Great Commission is concerned not with making disciples and baptizing them, but with teaching them everything that Jesus commanded us. Paul's aim was to teach *every* man in *all* wisdom, that he might present *every man* perfect in Christ (Col 1:28).

Even if you *have* heard of the "Four Spiritual Laws," they

[3]See pp. 136 ff.

are scarcely sufficiently exhaustive for this part of the program, whether or not they are adequate for evangelism, which in cultures influenced by Buddhism, Animism, Islam, Shintoism, etc., they rarely are! Those with a long Christian background who have had the rare privilege of sitting under a regular expository ministry may need less training than someone converted comparatively late, or who has had little systematic teaching and has sat under a grasshopping, impository or juxtapository type of preaching. A general knowledge not only of the whole Bible, but also of church history, systematic theology, Christian apologetics, etc., is obviously essential for effective evangelism and teaching, and the best way to get this for most people is to attend a well-recommended Bible college or seminary. This is required for training men for the home ministry and is no less essential for working overseas. Much fresh thinking is required before you can teach the Bible, not against the preconceptions of the culture in which you have been brought up, but against an entirely different set of cultural presuppositions. In India, for example, you could scarcely teach John's gospel without some idea of the concept of incarnation in Hinduism; nor in Japan about faith, without some knowledge of the Pure Land sects of Amida Buddhism; nor in any Buddhist country on the origins of evil without some understanding of and ability to distinguish between the Christian pluralist doctrine and the monistic view.

In a sample tribal catechism used among North Thailand tribal animists you may find an interesting approach. There is included the more traditional type of question-and-answer, memorized-by-rote type of catechism; but there is also included a story catechism where questions are asked on simple stories. For example, someone has become a Christian but their pig is lost; how can God have allowed this? The Christian doctrine of providence needs to be explained at this level. What will happen if the ancestral spirits are not worshiped? The story of the rich man and Lazarus gives you a starting point.

There are other problems that arise. We are so used to being Christians in a minority. But what teaching should be given where Christians form more than 50 percent of the population, as among the tribes of Assam or the Bataks of Northern Sumatra? You can scarcely suggest that politics is no concern of the Christian in that kind of situation; what the church is and does will inevitably have a profound effect on society as a whole! Read this extract from an article on a North Thailand situation:

> Nongwaen is nominally a Christian village, but the governing system of village law and custom is traditionally pagan. The moral life of the teenagers provoked the crisis. Since January six teenagers have had to be disciplined for immorality. Some mothers have been so concerned that for two months they met each morning at six o'clock in the church for prayer, while the church leaders exhorted the young people to lead pure lives. But their advice was rejected and parents increasingly lost authority over their teenage children. Some parents were unconcerned.
>
> *No easy solution.* Gway Seng asked if Scripture advocated a monetary fine by way of discipline. He felt that because the young people were not converted, Scriptural discipline had no "teeth", and thus they had no respect for it. Only a money fine, which hits at the roots of Yao materialism would prevent further immorality.
>
> Village meetings were called to discuss the problem. But what at first appeared to be a simple matter, the imposing of a fine for immoral conduct, began to snowball into a very complex matter. The rigid framework of Yao legislation would need altering. But this could lead to a "Pandora's box" situation unless changes were governed by the leading of the Holy Spirit. The imposition of a fine would affect the traditional pattern of Yao courtship, which involves promiscuity. The basic socio-economic work-group structure, which welcomes the children of unmarried daughters as potential workers, would be affected. House design would need revision and a different sleeping place would have to be found for the girls, who sleep alone near the back door for easy exit at night and

for lads to enter without disturbing the rest of the household. The whole social life of the teenagers would have to be revised, with acceptable substitutes introduced. Relationships with nearby non-Christian villages would have to be considered, since young lads "commute" looking for wives. Intrafamily relationships would need examining in the light of Scripture, since some parents feel no responsibility to discipline or supervise their children. Finally, the power structure in the village would be affected since the village leaders would need an authority over teenagers that could be enforced.[4]

This example shows just how much thinking has to be done, not just by armchair theologians at home, but by the pioneer missionary on a bamboo floor. It is a fallacy to suggest that any thickheaded, muscular Christian will do for pioneer work, as though such evangelism were a triumph of muscle over mind!

CHOOSING A PLACE FOR MISSIONARY TRAINING

There is a whole spectrum of institutions available in the various home countries, and these vary tremendously in traditions, standards, qualifications of the staff, and so on. In some colleges there is a strong overseas missionary emphasis; in others not really very much, and the emphasis is more on theology. Because of the vastly different situations in different home countries, it is difficult to give general advice. You would do best to get the advice not only of seniors whose opinions you value, but also, if possible, of contemporaries who have studied at the institutions in question.

In some countries there has been a tendency on the part of some university graduates to be highly critical of some of the Bible schools. These criticisms have had some foundation in the past. It is hard for an undergraduate who has been a free agent, making his own decisions like an adult, to submit him-

[4]David Griffiths, writing on North Thailand in the *East Asia Millions* (Nov. 1969).

self as a graduate to a system which treats him like a child.
Bible colleges are aware of the dangers of this kind of initiative-
stifling paternalism, which imposes external disciplines but
may not necessarily succeed in inculcating self-discipline. At
the same time, if one joined the armed forces for an earthly
battle, one would be subjected to equally irksome disciplines—
for a purpose. Thus I would strongly urge young graduates to
give the Bible colleges a break, and not to go on hearsay which
may be prejudiced and out-of-date, but to make serious inquir-
ies to discover what kind of contemporary courses are offered
today. Discipline may occasionally be irksome; it is not necessarily bad. Overseas there are many situations where one cannot just do as one likes, but must submit to the customs and
conventions of a different society. The "Why should I?" pro-
test cannot be allowed full expression if one is trying to adapt
to other cultures. The laissez-faire, let-everyone-do-what-is-
right-in-his-own-eyes "freedom"—very free relations with the
opposite sex, etc.—while highly contemporary, may be totally
unsuitable in many foreign cultures for a representative of
Jesus Christ.

The level of training aimed at usually depends upon the
abilities of the person concerned. If you are bright enough to
gain a higher theological degree then you should normally do
so, and this will mean going to a more academic type of institution. Sometimes the more academic institutions do not give
good practical training, and can be especially weak as far as
missionary training is concerned. This weakness needs to be
recognized and, in addition to studying academic theology, it
might be good to give a year to some specific missionary training course if such is available in your country. Many training
institutions are becoming increasingly flexible, seeking to provide more varied courses, and even to tailor courses to the
needs of the individual student. There are some good experi-

ments in progress, and there should be great improvements in the kind of missionary training available in the seventies.

ADVANCED THEOLOGICAL TRAINING

As national churches develop, nationals need to be trained for the ministry of the Word. One of the tragedies of evangelical missionary work has been that so often they have been satisfied with lower-level Bible schools instead of crowning these by providing theological teaching on the highest level. One reason has been the lack of sufficiently well-qualified missionaries. Out of some 1,500 evangelical missionaries in Japan recently, not one could be found who was competent enough in both languages to check a new Japanese translation against the original Hebrew. Liberals and Roman Catholics could have done it, but not Evangelicals. This suggests that a certain number of the finest theological brains ought to be prepared to give their services overseas. Having proceeded into postgraduate training (not necessarily to doctoral level initially, as this can be done later if required, and too long a delay makes integration and language-learning more difficult), they should get out and soak themselves in language and culture while still young enough to absorb it.

The expert who arrives on a sabbatical leave is far from unwelcome, but will be weak on application and may not understand some of his students' difficulties. The great need is for those who will come for a major portion of their lives. If it takes a good mind to lecture in theology at home, it takes a better one elsewhere in another language and another culture.

For those who are well qualified, it is certainly good to get in touch with those familiar with the needs in seminary-level teaching well ahead of time.

OTHER ACADEMIC DISCIPLINES

There are many situations where university graduates with a

good or an advanced degree may play a key part through evangelism in university and college situations. A recent writer, writing from a purely secular viewpoint, says, "The Teacher-Training Colleges are, in the modern world, as important as were the monasteries of mediaeval Europe."[5] And these should not be overlooked by those with degrees in education. There are considerable openings both through the Peace Corps and the various Voluntary Service Overseas schemes and the like.

In many countries in Africa and a few in Asia it is possible to teach in English. But in more highly developed countries like Japan, whereas expatriate teachers of English, German, or French conversation may be welcome, technical subjects are taught best by Japanese in their own language. There would be exceptions, of course, in the Nobel Prize-level class. In most Asian countries a language such as Chinese, Thai, or Indonesian needs to be well learned before you are able to teach in it. This means that a term of service in normal missionary work, living among the people of the land, may be the best preparation for understanding students in the academic community. In other places where "missions," as such, are not welcome, there can be a very real place for the "nonprofessional," and such persons have the advantage in countries where professional religious teachers, be they Buddhist, Christian, or whatever, are suspected of making money out of religion.[6]

BUSINESS QUALIFICATIONS

Just as with an army there are a considerable number of people concerned with transporting supplies, maintaining radio links, driving vehicles, supplying medical help, etc., so there are a variety of similar jobs which need doing to keep a body of missionaries on the field. Most of us are familiar with the various home representatives, candidates, and deputation

[5]Guy Hunter in *South-East Asia: Race, Culture and Nation* (London: Oxford U., 1966), p. 163.
[6]See chap. 8.

secretaries in the sending countries. There may be too many of these because of the multiplicity of missions, but missionaries need to have good communications with the churches in their home countries.[7]

It is less often realized that, in these days when governments employ large bodies of officials (in India something like one in every eighty-seven people is said to be a government official), a corresponding amount of work dealing with visas, work permits, reentry permits, income tax returns, etc., has to be undertaken on the field. Someone has to deal with this. Schools and hospitals, for example, have to order materials and correspond with the departments of education and health.

The group of missionaries to which I belong, for example, involves an annual budget of some million dollars a year. All these donations have to be properly acknowledged, expenses estimated, cash distributed, accounted for and audited. When missions are international and working in several countries, this means that they receive income in a dozen foreign currencies and spend it in another ten different currencies. Some of those currencies will be stable, and some anything but stable. Every year roughly a fifth of all missionaries are likely to make a return trip to their home countries, and this means visits to airline offices and the like. Protective inoculations have to be kept up.

The above facts make it clear that any large group of missionaries requires a trained accountant, a bookkeeper or two, some typists, and general factotum type of people, who will handle all these necessary matters. If they are properly trained, they can handle their jobs quickly and efficiently, and thus a few people can deal with all these necessary tasks, setting others free for more direct church-building work. But when such people are working, they nonetheless take every opportunity to play their own part in helping local Christians and working

[7]See chap. 9.

with local churches. There is thus a need for a small number
of people with business training of this kind. Medical and literature work also require some people with practical business
experience.

Such work should not in any sense be regarded as an inferior form of missionary endeavor. Missionaries can proceed
far better with their proper work if such work is done efficiently by those properly qualified to do it. All these workers are
part of the same body in action.

MEDICAL WORKERS

Work for doctors will vary greatly from place to place. There
are some who may be involved directly in small local clinic
work very closely and intimately connected with direct pioneer evangelism. Other doctors may be working in small general hospitals which demand considerable versatility of the
medical practitioner. Larger hospitals give opportunity for
men with various specialist qualifications, and there are of
course a few large Christian teaching hospitals. Even if there
is no medical student program, specialists are required in
hospitals where there is a proper nurses' training program.
If time is a problem for the busy doctor at home, it is an even
greater one in a missionary situation. If he is not very careful
and extraordinarily firm, the needs of the medical work will
first of all prevent him from getting an adequate control of
the language, apart from asking people to say "ah"! The tremendous medical need in many places is so great that if he is
not extremely firm and disciplined, his direct missionary purpose may become blurred and he may be forced into a situation
where he leaves the evangelism to others. Obviously there are
situations where this may be necessary, and yet it is a pity to
lose the greater impact of the direct witness of the man who is
actually giving physical help.

The work for nurses is extraordinarily varied. They may be

engaged in hospital work which gives them personal contact not only with the patients but also with nurses' aides and nurses in training. In some situations there may not be much bedside nursing; the work will tend to be primarily supervisory, involving training of nationals for nursing work. Outside the hospitals, there is often the work of smaller clinics which have shown themselves particularly effective in helping leprosy patients and in providing opportunities for direct evangelism and church-planting. Where there may be resentment against the evangelist who arrives with the sole specific purpose of proselytization, which may well be resented in a strong Muslim area, for example, the leprosy nurse has an appreciated reason for visiting in order to give positive help. If subsequently she stays to talk about the Lord, this is more acceptable. There is other work for nurses, of course, in starting Nurses' Christian Fellowship groups among national nurses. Missionaries themselves too often need help. Not only do missionary mothers need help in confinements, but when others fall sick it is a tremendous help if nurses are available to quietly run the home until mother recovers.

It is of course impossible to run a large hospital these days without pharmacists, lab assistants, radiographers, and people offering other forms of paramedical and technical assistance.

In all this it is desperately important that the main aim of a missionary society is borne in mind. It does not exist merely to bear a general witness to the love of Christ. This is a responsibility which all Christians have wherever they are and however they are employed. The aim of a mission hospital is to witness to the love of Christ in a practical way, and less directly to help in breaking down prejudice, and thus lead to the conversion of men and women in the planting and strengthening of local churches. There are some thrilling stories of the way in which African mission hospitals have been used to further this tremendous aim. Considerable numbers of Christians have been trained as medical assistants in scattered outpatient clinics, and many of these became nuclei of new little congregations. When there were no Christians to train initially, the impact has been smaller; but hospitals and clinics have had a widespread influence in opening people's hearts to the gospel. It is not that the work brings any obligation to embrace Christianity, but that the social concern of Christians is such as to break down the very strong prejudice against the Christian faith. Medical help is, of course, given to all indiscriminately, with no strings attached.

Linguists, Anthropologists and Researchers

There is, of course, a tremendous need for missionaries who are trained linguists. If they are going to engage properly in Bible translation they will also need a thorough knowledge of the biblical languages and an understanding of the theological issues involved. There are still very large numbers of languages in which the whole of the Bible is not yet available. It needs to be remembered that even when a version exists, there is a constant need for it to be brought up-to-date.

Apart from the general field of Bible translation, however, there is also the extremely important field of being able to help other missionaries in language-learning. The whole ministry of a missionary may be vitiated if his grasp of the language is poor. And the effectiveness of his ministry (while obviously depending primarily upon spiritual factors) is nonetheless much enhanced if his ability to speak and to use the language is developed to the utmost of his capacity. There is a further ministry here for the missionary linguist to help his fellow missionaries in their language training.

Missionaries also need to be sensitive to the extremes of cultural difference which may occur between different peoples. The availability of a trained anthropologist, especially in pioneer fields among little-known peoples, can be a tremendous advantage.

In order that missionary work may be fully informed, there is also a need for a limited number of people to be involved intimately in research. Such key personnel, who may be experts in fields like Islamics or in Buddhist studies, will be called upon not only for lecturing to theological students and conducting workshops for missionaries, but also for producing ideas for use in conveying the gospel through mass media and also supplying mission leaders with the information they require to make intelligent decisions.

LITERATURE WORKERS

It is very easy for us to take Christian literature for granted. Great strides in the quality and the range of materials available have been made in recent years in many home countries. But in some countries overseas the literature available is poorly produced and consists primarily of translations of material written with Western cultures in mind. The whole task, therefore, of training and encouraging national writers, of publishing good Christian literature, and finally (the greatest bottleneck of all) of building up an effective and wide distribution of such literature, is a worthy field of missionary endeavor.

Literature ministries are most effective when carried out in full integration with evangelism and church-planting programs. There is little use in producing materials which nobody wants to use. There is a very real danger that such programs, because of the finances involved, will be primarily directed by Westerners, and this is unfortunate. One hopes very much that the future trend will be for the development of fully national literature programs. There is still a very wide ministry in training fellow Christians in Christian writing, editing, publishing, distributing, and selling.

There is also a limited ministry for some, of course, in the writing and editing of material for the education of the Christian public at large about the work of the churches and their problems in other places. As is suggested later, there are probably too many missionary magazines, whereas a few magazines of absolutely first-rate quality would no doubt provide a far more effective information service to the churches at large.

Christian workers, therefore, with training in writing and journalism may have a particular contribution to make here in helping the churches of their home countries to become more aware of the needs and problems and the challenge of churches in other lands.

<h2 style="text-align:center">OTHER POSSIBILITIES</h2>

It does not seem possible in this book to outline all the possibilities which one could add to the above suggestions. Radio and television technicians, producers and scriptwriters are obviously much in the contemporary mode. But agriculturalists, physiotherapists, social workers, carpenters, builders, architects, and maintenance men also spring to mind. There seems virtually no end to the variety of training which may be of use in missionary situations.

At the same time, let us close this chapter by reminding ourselves that missionary societies exist for a certain specific and limited purpose. We must never lose sight of the end in view—to lead men and women to a living, personal faith in Jesus Christ. This means winning not only individuals but whole families, gathering them together into warm and welcoming congregations, and teaching and instructing them so that they become self-propagating and multiplying churches whose corporate life and testimony will bring the greatest glory to our Lord and Saviour Jesus Christ. This is why we placed the initial stress on the need for church-planters and lay trainers. Without their work the whole enterprise would lose its point.

4   Qualities: What It Takes

QUALITIES ARE MORE IMPORTANT than qualifications. In saying this I am not minimizing the value of scholarship or of training of all kinds, for scholarship is a great gain, and training a tremendous asset. Not all scholars make good missionaries or ministers, however, and not all training necessarily fits a man for service. A person may have all gifts and no graces. There are other men, with little scholarship and sometimes little training, who yet become most effective Christian workers.

This was more so perhaps in the days of Hudson Taylor, who opened the old China Inland Mission to those "of little formal education." In those days, university education in Britain was largely restricted to a select few who could go to Oxford or Cambridge, where non-Anglicans were still excluded. Without financial resources it was scarcely possible for even the most brilliant to get formal training. Today a very different situation exists. With the vast enlargement of the universities in most countries, and scholarships and state support for those with ability, it is rarer today to find a man of intellectual ability who has failed to get appropriate training. But there is more to qualities than a high IQ. A high IQ is rarely a disadvantage, and a low one is something of an encumbrance; but neither is a cause for either superiority or inferiority. "What do you have that you did not receive?" (1 Co 4:7, NASB) has a wide truthfulness. By the grace of God we are what we are, and we are not what we are not.

THE PREEMINENCE OF GRACE

I have known missionaries who were not very bright or beautiful (nevertheless the Lord God made them!), but who were effective because they were filled with the love of Christ; and the people to whom they went knew that they were loved. I have known some who were clueless about indigenous missionary principles and even tended to be a trifle paternalistic, but who got away with it because they loved and were known to love. I have known others, too, who failed to identify, and yet got away with it because of their warmth. First Corinthians 13 is true in all situations. Give me two missionaries, one with perfect language ability and no love, and the other with feeble language and yet with love, and I know which one will communicate Christ to those he meets. But one with good language ability and the love of Christ will communicate best.

It may seem self-evident, but when we talk of missionary preparation I would say from the heart that what we are shouts so much louder than all that we say or do. It is the fruit of the Spirit we need more than anything else. I have talked of training first, but all that is vain if we fail here. It is the spiritual which is preeminent. And this can come only as we seek Christ and come to Him, confessing our own emptiness and seeking His fullness. This does not mean that my tiny earthen vessel can contain Him, but that I seek to receive from Him "grace upon grace."

Ministers and missionaries are not supersaints, are not made of asbestos, but are subject to the same temptations as others (and, being in the forefront of the battle, are perhaps sometimes more fiercely tempted). If we are to represent our Master, if we are to be patterns for the emerging churches of how Christian men and women, fathers and mothers, wives and husbands, ought to live, then we need all the graces we can receive, and we can never have enough. It is this passion to grow in grace, to advance and progress in "wholeness" and Christlikeness, which should characterize the young missionary.

Missionaries need no pedestals. They are full of failings and have feet of clay; those who come out starry-eyed are due for disappointment. Yet the contrite, broken heart longing for holiness and Christlikeness must be there. The New Testament lists the things to be put off and the things to put on: "Fling off the dirty clothes of the old way of living . . . and . . . put on the clean fresh clothes" (Eph 4:24, Phillips). Such dress covers a multitude of sins, and no amount of training or scholarship is any substitute for these essential items on your spiritual supply list.

ATTITUDES

Racial superiority and nationalistic attitudes are the last things to be crucified. Most nations despise others and exalt themselves. To the Chinese only Chinese are people; others are various kinds of devils. Japanese missionaries probably have as big a problem crucifying their sense of racial superiority as most Westerners, and probably more.

There is nothing worse than the "them" and "us" mentality that one occasionally meets in some nonintegrated missionaries. One does sometimes still find an old "compound" with barbed wire on the walls, a gatekeeper to keep nationals out by day and bars on the windows to keep them out by night. Fortunately such places are mostly museum pieces by now, but the mentality can remain when the apparatus is removed. The wrong attitude may be found in people who are very dedicated professionals. The person who is too professional "works on them," the one who is dedicated may labor sacrificially "for them," but the need is for people who will work "with them," and think not of "them" so much as of "us." Our Master, friend of publicans and sinners, made a publican and a Samaritan the heroes of two of His most famous stories, and He did not hesitate to be with them Himself. If missionaries fail to be biblical in attitudes to race and class, the ministry is made a mockery (2 Co 6:3).

Someone has said that the hardest part about going to the

mission field is "the last eighteen inches." It is the unself-conscious identification which really counts. A Japanese missionary to Manchuria in the 1930s was beloved because when he went to the prison he sat where they sat, and "didn't even scratch." Others self-consciously squirmed among the vermin, but not he.

Identification is no easier today. Rising living standards in missionary-sending countries, in West or East, demand real effort on the part of those who have regarded washing machines, cars, a rich meat diet, refrigerators, and a handsome bathroom as normal. Why should I accept a lower living standard? No reason at all if you want to live like a spaceman in your own capsule and emerge periodically from your ivory tower to give out tracts, take a few prisoners, and return once more for a bath to get clean again!

> A people's soul is open only to the missionary who lives among them, and learns their language, their traditions, their customs, their ideas, and their values. If the missionary is indifferent to the culture in which he lives, if he pays no attention to public opinion in the local press (there are missionaries who do not take seriously the local newspapers), if he is not interested in the best literary and artistic expressions of that people, how can he know the thinking and the feelings of the people?[1]

Contrast this with an advertisement for a fully equipped house trailer for missionaries which

> provides all of the health safeguards available in the best hotel in the world . . . complete sanitary facilities, a water filter purifier system which delivers a gallon per minute of crystal clear water, a seven cubic foot refrigerator/freezer to protect his food, an air conditioning system to provide pure filtered air at all times. This is the best and certainly the least expensive health insurance a missionary and his family could possibly have.

[1]Emilio Nunez in his Urbana Address, 1967 (Chicago: Inter-Varsity, 1968), p. 290.

But I rather doubt whether that would help identification! It is possible for some missionaries to rush around giving out tracts, preaching through loudspeakers, and checking off a town as "evangelized" without ever going those last eighteen inches.

It is possible to preach an orthodox and biblical message couched in Western presuppositions without ever answering the problems of the hearers (because the missionary has never identified enough to realize that the problems exist). It can be shrugged off by saying the people are unresponsive or unreliable, when really it means that there has been a failure to communicate.[2]

WHAT AGE SHOULD MISSIONARIES BE?

The younger the missionary is, the more likely he or she is to adapt and identify. Recent average ages of new missionaries have been twenty-nine (Southeast Asia) and thirty (South America). Even so, a missionary who arrives abroad at these ages is already ecclesiastically senile in Asian cultures where 80 percent of the population is under thirty.

Youth is thus something of a priority. But all the stress on training tends to the later and later arrival of personnel on the field. There have been some attempts to get people out younger, giving them the very necessary additional training on subsequent furloughs. Twenty-two- and twenty-three-year-olds with real gifts and promise are worth taking a risk on. Maybe they are less well tried, and not everybody is mature at that age, and the moral risks may be greater, but the gain in identification and language-learning is worth it. Not that Bible training or church experience is unimportant or can be omitted; rather, the *sequence* in which such training is gained may be varied, and the person is exposed earlier rather than later to new language and culture. There are added advantages

[2]See chap. 7.

in that, instead of amassing degrees or training "in case it should be useful," people have an early exposure to the foreign situation and so gain a clearer idea of the task ahead and the best training to take.

In many countries the stress is still put on training and experience, which means older missionaries, but it would be worth training some younger ones. One Japanese group has sent out young men in their early twenties with some training to study as *students* in the Yeotmal Seminary in India. They learn to speak, eat, live, and think in Indian fashion. They grow up as equals with their Indian fellow students. After graduation they return to Japan, marry, and then return to India as missionaries, but with a degree of integration that they would not have had if they were only then entering India for the first time. Schemes like this would be worth developing.

What Place for Women Missionaries?

Sex is rather an important consideration. People occasionally talk foolishly or even disparagingly about women missionaries. Appeals for men often suggest that women are unwanted.

The fact is that, as 50 percent of the world's population remains female and as younger children can be effectively reached by women, it is scarcely surprising if there are more women missionaries than there are men. Some outstanding work has been done by some remarkable women missionaries, in spite of the fact that they do labor under some practical disadvantages.[3] In most Asian societies, for example, men are still dominant (in public at least) and it is they who make the decisions. It is men who take a lead in the churches also. In pioneer work the danger is that women missionaries may establish a women's meeting rather than a church, and it then becomes all the harder to develop a church from a women's

[3]We will say more about their special problems in chap. 6.

meeting. But there are a wealth of opportunities open to women. Married ones have much in common with their national sisters, who are curious about how they run their homes and bring up their babies. But of necessity they have less time to use for direct Christian work, and fewer free evenings. The single worker is single-minded in her devotion to the Lord, and is able to devote more time to direct Christian work.

Church work, Bible translation, hospital and clinic nursing, literature work, secretarial and bookkeeping work, catering, student work: there is plenty of scope for women workers.

PAUL AS A PATTERN MISSIONARY

It would not be an exaggeration to say that a great deal of the New Testament is a textbook of missionary attitudes. Certainly the Acts of the Apostles[4] and the epistles contain many helpful cameos of what a minister's life should be. It would sound absurd to say that such passages were more helpful to the missionary than to other Christians, but one cannot overlook the fact that the most direct application of some sections of Paul's epistles is to those engaged in work not so dissimilar to Paul's own work. The missionary cannot engage in Bible study without meeting continual challenges to the way in which he is carrying out his own ministry.

Some years ago I saw an article saying that Paul would have been turned down by the candidate committee of a modern missionary society because of his unimpressive presence, his contemptible speech, his bad health, his quarreling with a senior fellow worker, his continual stirring up of trouble with the civil authorities, his constant moving about and refusal to settle down and do a steady job of work, and so on! In fact, a study of his qualities and attitudes is most rewarding, although a thorough study would mean a detailed exposition of

[4]See *Missionary Ideals* by T. Walker of Tinnevelly, edited by D. C. C. Watson (London: Inter-Varsity, 1969) for a classic missionary study of Acts.

most of his epistles, in which there is such a wealth of personal reference.

One sometimes meets missionaries who never seem really to have unpacked. They have arrived, but somehow one gets the impression that they still have not quite made up their minds whether to leave their homeland permanently or not. Every furlough there seems a real possibility that they may not come back. Certainly the Lord at any time may redirect us, and there is nothing especially sacrosanct about serving on one side of a stretch of water rather than on another. I am not trying to suggest that "service for life" is the only really spiritual possibility (although in chap. 7 on cross-cultural communication, reasons are given why long-term service is much better than short-term). But there are people who never seem to have committed themselves completely to the course of action upon which they have embarked.

Paul showed a characteristic wholeheartedness in all that he did, even in persecuting Christians before his conversion (Ac 9:1-2). He never seemed to go in for half measures. What he was prepared to endure is revealed in his "boasting" to the Corinthian church in 2 Corinthians 11:23—12:9.

> Five times I received from the Jews thirty-nine lashes. Three times I was beaten with rods, once I was stoned, three times I was shipwrecked, a night and a day I have spent in the deep. I have been on frequent journeys, in dangers from rivers, dangers from robbers, dangers from my countrymen, dangers from the Gentiles, dangers in the city, dangers in the wilderness, dangers on the sea, dangers among false brethren; I have been in labor and hardship, through many sleepless nights, in hunger and thirst, often without food, in cold and exposure. Apart from such external things, there is the daily pressure upon me of concern for all the churches. Who is weak without my being weak? Who is led into sin without my intense concern? (11:24-29, NASB).

None of these sufferings made him give up. This is the spirit that we find again and again—the desire that "Christ will be honored in my body, whether by life or by death" (Phil 1:20, RSV). He sees his body as an instrument in the hand of God, for Him to use. The Japanese colloquial version of Philippians 1:12 runs, "The things that have happened to my body have turned out, contrary to what you might expect, for the advance of the gospel." He saw his body and his life as media by which Christ's glory might be revealed and the gospel advanced. It is this passion to preach Christ and to plant churches, whatever it may cost, and to go on doing it while breath remains, which is the authentic apostolic spirit. So easily we can come with our conditions: "We will follow you, Lord, but—" and there are various assurances that we would like first. Those who are our seniors grew up in a world where nothing was guaranteed. We, however, having experienced something of what today's affluent society has to offer, have come to regard certain things as our expected due and to feel that life is scarcely tolerable unless they are provided. Do we have this same unconditional abandonment to the cause of Jesus Christ and the same passion to make Him known as Paul had? Let us pray for it.

Do not misunderstand me. A sense of shrinking from the unknown is normal. If, like me, you are the kind of person who cannot read a medical advertisement without thinking you have got the disease, you will naturally wonder about all the diseases you might catch abroad. Even the fearless Moses said, "Send, I pray, some other person." We recognize that same shrinking from the unknown. The missionary challenge to be willing "to go anywhere" can cause us some anxiety. To be frozen to death in the Arctic, to die of cholera in India, to be killed by the hands of brigands in China, to die of thirst or snakebite in the tropics—am I willing for all this, I wonder? Fortunately all these alternatives are mutually exclusive! We do not have to screw up courage to go to all the terrible places that we can imagine, but only to one particular place. After we have been there and come to share the life of other people (who after all live there, as well as die there), we wonder what we were worrying about. The great thing about the unknown is that once we have arrived there, it is unknown no longer.

A CERTAINTY OF DIVINE CALLING

Does it surprise you, after the emphasis of the first chapter upon objective guidance, that a certainty of divine calling should be stressed? But it is there in Scripture, and it cannot be omitted. To go as a missionary merely because others think you should go is totally inadequate. When the going becomes difficult, if we are there only because friends or a committee or a pressing missionary have sent us, then we shall be very ready to change our mind and to go home again.

We cannot read about Paul without realizing this very deep sense he has of divine commissioning. We notice that his conversion was, certainly in its outward manifestations, a more remarkable one than normal, and we may feel that his special place as an "apostle of Christ" is a factor which cannot be forgotten. But we may still believe that such a sense of God's calling and commissioning (as with the Old Testament prophets) is important. The word to Ananias (Ac 9:15) was that Paul was "a chosen instrument of mine." Paul himself could say, "But when He who had set me apart, even from my mother's womb, and called me through His grace, was pleased to reveal His Son in me, that I might preach Him among the Gentiles I did not immediately confer with flesh and blood" (Gal 1:15-16, NASB). Writing to Timothy, he says, "According to the glorious gospel of the blessed God, with which I have been entrusted . . . He considered me faithful, putting me into service" (1 Ti 1:11-12, NASB).

A man or a woman must know as they go forth that they have been chosen and commissioned by God Himself to preach. This is more important than any human ordination and commissioning. We need that same inner constraint: "For if I preach the gospel, I have nothing to boast of, for I am under compulsion; for woe is me if I do not preach the gospel" (1 Co 9:16, NASB).

A DEEP CONCERN FOR THE LOST

This used to worry me as a student: Why did I not have an overwhelming burden for the salvation of non-Christians? I began to realize that as a student my main task was not evangelism, but to glorify God in my work. If I had been given the depth of concern that I, at that time, felt was appropriate, I would have done nothing but personal evangelism. The concern was there, but was commensurate with the opportunities available to a full-time Christian student. But the concern is one that deepens when in contact with the situations overseas where believers are so very few and when one sees the hopelessness and emptiness of nonchristian lives in the mass to an extent that is less possible in places where Christian influence has been strong.

When Paul saw people in Athens wholly given to idolatry, for all the great intellectual traditions of that city, his spirit was "provoked within him" (Ac 17:16, NASB). As Christ's ambassador he entreated men, "We beseech you, . . . be reconciled to God" (2 Co 5:20, RSV). His great concern, although the apostle to the Gentiles, was for the conversion of his fellow countrymen also: "I have great sorrow and unceasing grief in my heart. For I could wish that I myself were accursed, separated from Christ for the sake of my brethren, my kinsmen according to the flesh" (Ro 9:2-3, NASB). "My heart's desire and my prayer to God for them is for their salvation" (Ro 10:1, NASB). He went on to say, "How then

shall they call upon Him in whom they have not believed?
And how shall they hear without a preacher?" (Ro 10:14,
NASB) .

It is not easy *in vacuo,* I know, to realize this. The Lord
could say to Moses, "I have seen the affliction of my people
. . . and have heard their cry. . . . I know their sufferings" (Ex
3:7, RSV) , but our problem is that we are far removed from
that kind of situation. And while mass media help us to know
more, we can become hardened even to pictures of the needs of
men. God knows and hears and sees, but we so often forget.

Theological vagueness and speculation may have weakened
men's concern for those without Christ; we need to recalibrate
our thinking and our attitudes with the Bible. Paul had no
doubts about men's desperate need of salvation, and his sense
of compulsion about men in the grasp of Satan was also in-
tensified by his own certainty that all of us must stand before
the judgment seat of Christ for His objective and absolute
verdict upon the things we have done in the body, whether
they are bad or good. Paul goes on: "Therefore, knowing the
fear of the Lord, we persuade men" (2 Co 5:11, NASB) . It is
not only that men have a deep need, but that I am answerable
for whether or not I have really sought to meet men's need.

HUMILITY

There may have been a day (though I doubt it) when the
"great white chief" syndrome was acceptable in missionary
candidates, but certainly the new missionary today needs to
come in the role of a learner, as much as in that of a teacher.
Even today one does meet young missionaries who, having been
to Bible school and educated from Halley's *Bible Handbook*
and Torrey's *How to Work for Christ* (excellent books both
of them) , now see themselves as coming out to "head up" the
work, and to show the ignorant nationals how to do it. The
brash assumption is made that the way things are done in

one's home country must of necessity be the best way of doing it. This is really a painful form of provincialism which can be especially painful to national brethren. Such a missionary can be a real test of the sanctification of a national leader. When such missionaries try to assert their leadership, if a national explodes, he may be quite wrongly accused of being "anti-foreign." We need to realize that some of those to whom we go may be better educated academically and theologically than we are, and be willing to go as learners.

Thus Paul speaks of "serving the Lord with all humility" (Ac 20:19, NASB) and describes himself as "the very least of all saints" (Eph 3:8, NASB). One is amazed and then delighted that the cultured, intellectual Jewish rabbi and Roman gentleman can call the runaway slave Onesimus "a beloved brother, especially to me" (Phile 16, NASB). When Paul had been slapped by order of the high priest and was speaking out against the illegality of this, it was pointed out to him that he had reviled God's high priest. He at once apologized, "I did not know" (Ac 23:1-5, Williams).

WIDTH OF KNOWLEDGE

In these days of increasing specialization there is a danger that people may be rather ignorant outside their own field of knowledge. This danger is a real one for the theological student and for the missionary. Yet, in the nature of his work, a missionary needs not only to be an expert in his own subject—that is in *the* Book—but also to have the widest knowledge of the language and culture of the country to which he goes. He needs a real breadth of reading; he will have to meet people from all walks of life, and it will be of great value if he can take an informed interest in them. I remember one train journey in Japan when my neighbors' interests included marine biology, a rare geological phenomenon thought to be due to large meteorites, and the films of an outstanding Japanese movie producer, whose name I am ashamed to say I have forgotten. It was this subject which led via *Ben Hur* to talking of the gospel.

Paul could speak to Jews and show a complete familiarity with the Scriptures. He could also speak to Greeks against the background of their own literature and culture. He did not deliver a diatribe against idolatry on a basis of the Jewish Scriptures, but reasoned about the futility of this "ignorance" on a basis of their own presuppositions, although he was no less authoritative in proclamation. Certainly Paul's varied educational background, including the school of Gamaliel as well as the Greek culture of Tarsus, was a great help to him. Some Christians grow up in a narrow and restricted circle and can be very intolerant, to the point of appearing ignorant. I once felt very embarrassed in a committee of Japanese to hear them say of a missionary of another fellowship, who had been criticizing them, "We have to face the fact that Mr. X is a simple-minded man and doesn't see the problem"! This was the kindest way it could have been put. Paul possessed the breadth of mind to write Romans 14, advising tolerance on nonessentials. (We must not forget, however, that he stood very firm when essential Christian doctrine and principles were at stake.) Occasionally one hears the opinion expressed that it would be wrong for someone to go abroad as a missionary, because his abilities are too good to be wasted. A man like Henry Martyn, even though he died so young, was not wasted; it took a mind like his to produce translations of the whole New Testament in three languages before dying at the age of thirty-one.

PRACTICAL ABILITY

In many situations, men who are capable of doing many practical jobs are much appreciated. A Polynesian church gazette listed qualifications as:

Ability to mix with people, mix concrete, wade rivers, write articles, love one's neighbour, deliver babies, sit cross-legged, conduct meetings, drain swamps, digest questionable dishes, patch human weaknesses, suffer fools gladly, and burn midnight oil.

It went on to suggest that

persons allergic to ants, babies, beggars, chop suey, cockroaches, curried crabs, duplicators, guitars, humidity, indifference, itches, jungles, mildew, minority groups, mud, poverty, sweat and unmarried mothers had better think twice before applying.

Pioneer situations can be the most demanding in this regard, but even in an established work there is great value in being able to repair cars, use tools, type, play a musical instrument, and so on. Paul was a tentmaker and stayed with Aquila and Priscilla because he was "of the same trade." (The rabbis, although scholarly intellectuals, were nonetheless expected to learn a trade.) Carey the shoemaker is another model. This writer is not too well endowed in this direction, and fortunately has never had to be, except in areas such as gardening, shovelling snow, and so on, but one is ever envious of the fellow missionary who knows how to make things.

"Paul had gathered a bundle of sticks" (Ac 28:3, NASB) is a pleasing cameo of the great apostle, shipwrecked but far from being an idle, listless prisoner. He had to do something to help and get everyone warm in that cold, rainy weather. This may seem a prosaic note on which to end a chapter on missionary qualities, and yet it ensures that we are down to earth in our thinking.

5 Logistics: What It Costs

You can't get away from money. Missionaries have digestive systems just like other people, and they have to be fed a reasonable number of calories. Living abroad, they cannot afford to live like tourists in hotels, but their daily bread still costs something. They need clothes too—and sometimes it is a joke to see how far behind they get with fashions. But if you wear temperate-weather clothes only once every five years, they tend not only to smell of mothballs, but also to last longer than other people's! The aim of this chapter is to help prospective missionaries to "count the cost."

Cost of Training

Whereas secular education these days, in Britain at least, is generally available on a basis of government-provided funds for those with the necessary preliminary educational aptitude, Bible and theological training is not always to be obtained so readily. Training for the ministry of denominational churches is usually provided by those churches on a basis of grants and scholarships of various kinds, but it is not always possible to get such help for independent colleges, although it is sometimes possible to apply for grants. If grants are not available, it means that someone wanting to go abroad needs to spend time in secular employment, saving hard in order to get enough money to pay his own college expenses. This is one reason why some study later rather than earlier, and arrive abroad later rather than earlier, with the consequent increased difficulty in integration. In New Zealand and Japan I know of churches that help their own young people through such Bible training, which is a trend to be encouraged. In North America many

70

have to earn their living by doing part-time work while they are studying, both in universities and Bible colleges and seminaries. Systems vary from country to country. But this provides a useful test of dependence upon the Lord for the supply of financial needs in answer to prayer, by whatever channel He may choose to supply it.

Cost of Passages and Travel

Many missionary societies still follow the ancient traditions of getting potential candidates to pray in their "passage money," while others have no such proviso. It does need to be recognized, though, that traveling around the world is expensive business. Travel by passenger ship is becoming increasingly more expensive than travel by cheaper charter flight, or even at economy rates on the standard airlines. But the probability is that, in an average missionary life of about twenty-five years, five return trips will be made. With a wife and family to pay for as well, the cost of even one return trip to "the field" is a formidable sum. Most people on a normal income would have to save for many years before they could afford such a journey.

Why stress a point like this? In order to make it plain that the cost to the churches of meeting such travel is very high indeed. Many missions have understandings that people who do not complete a tour of service may have to refund some proportion of the cost of their travel. Stewardship of funds must be watched most carefully. We are not to join a mission and see the world at the expense of the sacrificial giving of old-age pensioners and others who can little afford it, but who yet give generously for the Lord's work.

Cost of Living

It is hard to understand the irresponsibility of some congregations who may commend members for overseas service or be prepared to call people "our missionaries," and yet make little effort to find out what it actually costs to maintain a missionary in a particular foreign country. It cannot always be true these days that the cost of living is cheaper abroad than at home. In countries such as Japan and Ghana it may well be higher, especially in cities, and the missionary's problem is how to keep up with the rising standard of the people among whom he is working. The increasing urbanization, and the consequent increasing deployment of missionaries in strategic cities, means that the cost of rented accommodations is steadily rising (in the Far East of late by approximately 25 percent per year). The cost of buying houses is often prohibitive.

Missionary societies differ a great deal in what they consider to be the "normal" provision made for missionaries. The figures given vary tremendously, and a great deal may seem to go for "overhead." This does not necessarily represent any inefficiency in management. In these days when people live much longer, a missionary may serve for thirty years and then continue to require support for a thirty-year retirement! The costs of passages and education of children must also be reckoned, as well as the great costs of various forms of work in institutions such as hospitals and language schools, and in religious broadcasting and television. Strangely enough, however, people often seem far more prepared to give for medical work (a very concrete form of well-doing) than for evangelism.

The advertised cost of supporting a single missionary of an international mission for twelve months at a lower-level living standard runs from rock bottom $1,200 (£500) a year to a more normal average $2,400 (£1,000) a year, but "faith" missions may not always be able to maintain what they regard as "normal." Some wealthier missions, especially the denominational ones, may pay far higher remittances, though this undoubtedly is widely criticized as a failure to adapt their standard of living to local conditions in many Africasian countries. This problem is a real one, for though missionaries may be receiving far less than their contemporaries in a home ministry, nationals do not know this, and it is all too easy for the missionary to appear affluent to the point of luxury.

EXTRA COSTS

It needs to be appreciated that missionaries face many extra costs because they are missionaries, which they would not have to bear at home. This is especially true for those who have grown up in a socialized state and who expect that all educational and medical needs will be met by the state. They may well not be in another country. I know one American missionary who belongs to a mission which asks for pledged support before return to the field. He had six children all attending the Christian Academy in Japan (a private Christian secondary school run on American lines; the secular American school was more expensive still!). Such was the cost of schooling that this poor man had to find people who could promise him altogether a total of $1,100 a month—or an annual salary of $13,200 (£5,500), which is no mean salary by any standard. Few local churches can afford to support such a missionary, but this is one of the problems of education on the field.

Coming from Great Britain to the Far East we were early impressed with medical costs, and hit $60 worth of medical expenses in our first two weeks in Japan. (The Lord in His goodness had sent a special gift of exactly that sum for us the week before we got there!) Having babies can be an expensive business (the British government grants to citizens abroad are generous, but do not cover expenses), while major surgery can be so expensive that it may be cheaper for some to fly home.

This situation differs depending on home countries. Furlough missionaries in North America face the heaviest medical and dental bills. I even knew a woman missionary who used part of her small remittance to pay a small insurance premium each month; she was insuring herself against the expense of dying in the United States! This, as the world knows from *The American Way of Death,* can be an extremely expensive business.

Mention of insurance reminds me that missionaries can rarely afford to insure their belongings against theft and damage, so that a burglary or flood may cause unanticipated hardship which would not hit people at home quite so hard.

The Life of Faith has drawn attention to the costs of getting children out to the field in summer vacations to see their missionary parents. It is certainly cheaper for children to study in their own home countries, and makes it easier for them to integrate in their own environment, but for the parents the separation from their children is a real hardship. Getting children out to see their parents even every alternate year is another additional cost. Nonchristian organizations often bring such children out every year or more often.

FINANCIAL PRINCIPLES

It is often pointed out that, however money is found, all missions are "faith missions," though the term is very much out of favor. It is certainly true that, whether mention of needs is made publicly or not, all Christians alike depend on the Lord for the supply of their needs.

In recent years, with the increasing number of missionary societies and with the introduction of what some would regard as "sensible business methods" and others as "carnal worldly promotion," there has been a sad spirit of competitiveness. This seems totally inappropriate for Christian organizations, since all are members of the same body of Christ. Things have reached a sorry state when a mission's receipts are alleged to reflect the efficiency of a fund-raising specialist or of a public relations consultant who knows to a nicety what kind of "soft sell" to use, what kind of harrowing photograph to employ. It seems highly doubtful whether the slickness of the advertising and publicity handouts should really be the factor which determines whether a certain part of the world receives more missionaries, or more money for them to use. The worst aspect is that apparently so few see anything incongruous in the adoption of business terminology for Christian work. In this "rat race" many groups which once were careful to avoid making financial appeals have felt obliged to find some human way of trying to increase their income.

While it can certainly be argued that making needs known publicly is not of necessity less spiritual than refraining from making them known, there are some indications from the New Testament, said by many to be their "only rule of faith and conduct," as to how such matters should be conducted. Even where some would argue that the New Testament does not give a blueprint for every situation at every period in history, one cannot but observe that all Christians are urged not to be anxious about what they eat, drink, or put on, and not to be anxious about tomorrow. This is the attitude of "the Gentiles," but not of those who belong to the kingdom of heaven; our sure trust is in a heavenly Father who knows what we need. This attitude does seem to preclude purchasing address lists of wealthy Christians known to be generous in bestowing their money! The apostle Paul, while perfectly prepared to appeal for money for others, and to accept the gifts which churches sent to him, would rather work with his own hands than ask money for himself. The noncompetitive faith-mission approach does, then, seem to have some validity.

On the other hand, Christians have a stewardship which they wish to exercise, and it is difficult to see how they can do this responsibly without a certain minimum of information! Some ways need to be found whereby Christians who wish to

gain information may obtain it. There is a great deal of difference between constant panic appeals for funds, almost
amounting to declarations of debt and insolvency, and giving
an objective report of what funds have been received *and* of
how they have been spent. The custom of merely publishing
receipts seems meaningless unless people have some idea how
many people this sum has to support. The average set of
audited accounts means very little to anybody except a trained
accountant.

To those who are sufficiently concerned to read a mission
magazine, or to request prayer material, there would seem no
direct solicitation involved in giving diagrammatical explanations of how money is spent, and to give some indication of
the relation between what was budgeted for and what was actually received. In making your choice of a missionary society,
it is worthwhile giving thought to this financial aspect in order
to decide which approach seems most appropriate and scriptural to you.

Church Responsibility

So-called "faith principles" have been most misleading when
they have been made an excuse by the local church or assembly
for shrugging off their responsibilities by assuring everyone
that "the Lord will provide" the needs of the missionaries, and
so nothing more need be done. It cannot be too strongly
stressed that "faith principles" refer to the attitude of the re-
cipient receiving thankfully from the Lord whatever He sends,
learning both to be abased and how to abound. It should
never be used to excuse churches from their responsibility to
provide in an informed and adequate way for the missionaries
which they send out.

If, as has been suggested earlier, churches are going to be
encouraged to be far more deeply involved in the sending out
of missionaries, then a more realistic shouldering of financial

responsibilities should be one by-product of this. But how again is this to be effected, especially if you belong to a church with its own denominational society and you wish to serve with some interdenominational fellowship? It seems all wrong to go ahead and get accepted by any society without proper reference to your own local congregation. More responsible missionary societies will probably want to establish a closer link with the sending church in any case, but even if they do not, you should insist on it.

There may well be questions about your reluctance to go out with the accepted denominational mission. If their doctrinal position is unacceptable, then you should be prepared to stand on your personal convictions and say so. If they are not working in the part of the world to which you feel a strong personal sense of call, this might be a more acceptable reason to them. But we should be honest, and be prepared to do our utmost to involve our own home church from the very beginning in our own going forth. A mere good reference from our minister is not enough. We should endeavor to secure, if possible, the approval of the whole congregation, or at least of its elders and deacons. In such a way the whole church becomes personally involved in missionary work through you, and not merely impersonally through giving to fulfill a quota due to the support fund of some depersonalized set of initials.

If this seems a council of perfection to some students or nurses away from home whose formal church connections have become tenuous, may I urge that, if you are going to take the local church seriously overseas, and to expect others to do the same and to accept its discipline, you should be prepared to take the local church seriously yourself at home now. You may feel that there is little New Testament authority for any "membership" of a local congregation, that therefore you are a member of any true congregation of Christ's people, and "in fellowship" wherever you go. But not all may share this viewpoint, least of all the church which you attend. Even in student days, then, it would seem important to make it clear to the responsible church leaders that you want to belong to the church in the fullest possible sense and not to be regarded merely as a "student visitor." If your attendance at your "home" church is going to be restricted to four or five visits a year, and you can anticipate spending several years attached to a hospital, college, or university in another city, it would seem far better to reach a definite understanding with both your home church and the church in the city where you spend most of your time. This is a matter which congregations in large cities with hospitals or institutions of higher learning ought to take seriously, by seeking to establish closer relationships with student members of the congregation.

ATTITUDES TOWARD POVERTY

It is hurtful to one's pride to be an object of charity. Even though the Bible does say that the laborer deserves his wages, though the Old Testament enunciates the principle and exemplifies it in the Levites, and though the Lord endorses it Himself, it still can be hurtful to be made to feel dependent on others. Others are sometimes singularly untactful. It is hard to know which is worse—to be handed a check in an envelope the moment a service is over, as though you had preached in order to gain an honorarium, or to be asked how much your traveling expenses were and to be given it in change from the collection plate! None of us likes to feel we live on the charity of others. But it is good that pride should be wounded. If we accept what we receive as from the Lord, it will help us to accept gifts gladly and with real thankfulness to Him and to the donors.

You will need to accept the fact of being poor. It makes little difference if you belong to a so-called faith mission or to one which appeals for funds. In either event the probability is that you will always have to be careful with money (and there is no great harm in that!). It is not that you will not have enough; we always get what we "need," and often, through the generosity of others, far more than we need.

So do not think that you will avoid temptations to covetousness by becoming a minister or an overseas missionary. You do not need to be wealthy to be covetous. "Even in missionary flesh there dwells no good thing," as someone wryly remarked! It may be that some other misisonary gets more personal gifts and can afford more personal indulgences. Or there may be the far greater struggle when, each time you take a furlough, you see what you have renounced by choosing treasure in heaven rather than on earth. When you see the affluence of friends and relatives in homes, cars, and vacations, it is hard not to be able to buy your wife the clothes you would like to see her wear, and even harder to feel that the children are inadequately supplied compared with their playmates at school. It is good to face up to these things early, to settle before the Lord your own willingness to be abased and to rejoice in your poverty "as poor yet making many rich, as having nothing yet possessing all things" (2 Co 6:10, NASB).

In any case those of us who take such a path can rarely feel virtuous and tell the Lord all that we are putting up with for His sake! He so often surrounds us with blessings which far more than meet all our needs—and spares us all the financial worry of those who have so much tax to pay! But settle this before God, and marry a man or woman who has accepted it also; otherwise you will not last long. It is irresponsible to let others bear the expense of investing in training you, and then waste it all by giving up halfway to the goal.

TRUSTING GOD

I always enjoy Hudson Taylor's words to members of the old China Inland Mission:

> Every member of the Mission is expected to recognize that
> this dependence for the supply of all his need is on God, who
> called him, and for whom he works, and not on the human
> organization . . . their faith must be in God, their expectation
> from Him. The funds might fail or the Mission might cease to
> exist, but if they put their trust in Him He will never fail nor
> disappoint them.

It would certainly be the testimony of the present writer,
borne out by our own family experience and by that of our
friends and fellow missionaries, that the Lord is constantly
surprising us with His kindness and the miraculous nature of
His provision at crucial times. We have remarked that whenever we have obeyed the injunction that "it is better to give
than to receive," and have made a special gift over and above
our regular giving, the Lord returns it to us through some other
channel, almost to the point of embarrassment.

Thus we can only say to potential missionaries: Do not
worry about money. God is faithful to His promises and does
not let us trust Him in vain. It is good to learn to do this in
early years, and to learn to pray for needs now; this strengthens
our faith. The Lord is not bound to any one method; different
people's needs are met in differing ways. For a few He may
provide through a private income or family legacies, for others
through a business organization, for others through a mission
which pays regular salaries, for others through missions which
make no guarantees but equally divide what the Lord sends
the whole group, while others may go out independently,
trusting directly in the Lord to respond to their own faith. But
the testimony of us all is that God does care for us and provides
not only for our needs and our daily bread, but often an extra
slice of cake as well.

Each intending missionary or minister needs to come to a
settled attitude of mind on this subject, but the whole matter
can be summed up in these words:

God is able to provide you with every blessing in abundance, so that you may always have enough of everything *and* may provide in abundance for every good work. . . . He . . . will supply *and* multiply your resources and increase the harvest of your benevolence (2 Co 9:8-10, RSV marg.).

6 *Marriage, Children, or Neither?*

THERE ARE OTHER KINDS of costs besides the financial ones described in the previous chapter. I remember asking a lady
missionary, "Well, did you have a good furlough?" and she
said, "Do you want the truth? Not really." And I understood
why. It is hard when one's parents have died, and one goes
home. One still has friends and goes gladly around to see
them. But after two or three hours the conversation has caught
up on all the gossip about mutual friends and begins to slacken,
and one realizes that the others have their own lives to live.
Other single women have their own apartments and their own
local circle of acquaintances. But the missionary has only some
temporary quarters, has been away perhaps for twenty years or
more, apart from furlough visits, and somehow each time of
furlough seems to know fewer people. It needs to be realized
that there is a very real cost to be paid in loneliness in later
years. Although we are returning to our native country, often
we seem to belong to it less and less and feel more at home
in our adopted land.

WILLINGNESS TO BE UNMARRIED

Of those who remain single, some are unmarried by choice
and by a God-given conviction. Others have had it thrust
upon them by force of necessity. There is a great deal of difference between the settled peace of heart of a girl in one of
the German Protestant deaconess orders who knows that normally, once she has been accepted (around the age of twenty-
seven or twenty-eight), she will then remain unmarried, and
those who are always yearning for a change and who each time

they go on furlough hope that somebody might turn up.[1]

This is a real problem which demands sympathetic understanding by friends. Relatives, especially mothers perhaps, often make it no easier because they, understandably enough, are always hoping to arrange something.

Sometimes the Lord removes the sense of want and longing for marriage; other women have to live with it all their lives. Some can get joy vicariously in enjoying other people's children; others have to put up walls to protect themselves. Others compensate by becoming hypercritical of the consecration of their married sisters. Some have to face the danger of the wrong kind of affection for members of the same sex.

Does it seem hard to mention these matters now? It is good that they should be faced realistically in advance. Perhaps this is impossible. We may be so certain of our own uniqueness that we can still tuck away a belief that "it will be different for me" when we think we are being realistic. At least we have a responsibility, I believe, to warn younger people that the loneliness of middle age and old age for single people is made no easier by living overseas and having no settled base. If you are an effective missionary, then the probability is that you will be asked to train other younger missionaries. In that case you may have to share your own home with a succession of different younger women, to each of whom you will have to adapt afresh.

Christ refers to those who are single "for the sake of the kingdom of heaven" and Paul speaks of those who are able to have a single-minded devotion to Christ. Happy are those who are able to hold joyously to such a calling. And it should be seen as a calling, rather than as an unfortunate necessity.

In this context it is helpful to notice the attitude of the German order of deaconesses mentioned above, expressed in the following translation:

---

[1]See Helen Roseveare, *Give Me this Mountain* (London: Inter-Varsity, 1966) for a frank and first-hand account of this problem.

We know that fulfilment and meaning in life are given to us through Jesus Christ. Under His leading we take both want and abundance from God's hand. Marriage as well as celibacy we regard as equal status before God to which He calls His disciples (female as well) according to His will.

We see in the call to deaconesses at the same time the call to celibacy which we receive gratefully as a gift and affirm whole-heartedly (Jn. 10:10b; Mt. 19:10-12; I Cor. 7:25-28, 32, 34, 35).

1. We are quite aware of the fact that even with the call to celibacy the continued "I will" to it will not be without its tests.

2. But we trust that as the Lord Jesus gives the call to celibacy He has also ready for us the power to overcome temptation by His Word and through the Holy Spirit, which we may use by faith.

In the ensuing prayer there is:

Thanksgiving

For the knowledge that our life has found fulfilment in the redemption of His Son.
For the calling to life and service in celibacy and for the resulting freedom to meet special opportunities in service.
For the strength to overcome the problems which sometimes arise from celibacy.

Repentance and confession

Dissatisfaction, unhappiness and lack of authority are evidences of the fact that we have not mixed our calling with faith and have not said our daily fresh "I will" but have, due to side-glancing on the ways of life of others, brought ourselves to waver. The resulting dissatisfaction renders the testimony of our life doubtful. We confess this and bend low.[2]

The point that emerges is that there is great peace of mind in settling that a single life is a "calling" from the Lord and not a "cross" to be borne.

[2]Quoted with permission from *Mit Freuden Dienen* (*With Joyous Service*), the Life-rule of the Deaconesses of the Puschendorf Motherhouse.

MARRIAGE: PROS AND CONS

In most countries overseas, marriage is normal, and good parents always try to arrange marriages for their children. The single person is not understood. Nationals are convinced that there must have been a partner sometime, or there still is somewhere. The earthy biological facts of life demand it. It seems hard to believe that a family would be so irresponsible and inconsiderate as not to arrange a marriage for their children, however ill-favored.

Because marriage is the accepted norm, therefore, the married person is best understood and the unmarried least. Mothers have common ground at once with the wives and mothers in their new environment. This is something which, for all her foreign strangeness, she shares with them. Nonetheless, the single missionary has some advantages:

1. The married person has many responsibilities which keep him or her tied down. Paul's words in 1 Corinthians 7:32-35 make it plain that the uncommitted person may be much freer to give his or her time to working for the gospel and for the growth of the church. A mother is tied to her small children; the father cannot be away too much. Even when the children are older, parents need to make sure that they are available to spend time with them during the school vacation. There are limits imposed by nursing babies, staying with them in the evenings, keeping them amused, cared for, dressed and fed.[3] (Even while writing part of this chapter, the writer was rocking a baby's cradle with one foot!)

2. While having a babe in arms and learning a language are not by any means mutually exclusive alternatives, sometimes several small children in the toddling stage make study all but impossible. This means that a wife has a very difficult

[3]For an excellent and most helpful book on the problems of missionary mothers see J. T. Tuggy, *The Missionary Wife and her Work* (Chicago: Moody, 1966).

job learning a language seriously once a family starts to grow.

3. Identification and acculturation are always easier for the unmarried. He or she can more easily join a national household for some months and so get much closer than the family that requires their own home, and makes it a little bit of "olde England" or "little ole USA." At conferences, too, a married couple will have a room of their own; the single man or girl can live in a dormitory with the young people, listening to conversation under the blankets until the small hours of the morning.

4. In pioneer work a single man is freer to travel extensively and be away on long trips.

Thus there are valid reasons for postponing marriage, provided that these are fully understood by both parties and accepted by both. If delay is a strain, then it is better to marry, though a case can still be made for delaying the arrival of children.

As a final word, it is interesting to note that it is not only Christians who may recommend delay to serve a cause. The following is a letter to the China *People's Daily:*

> We feel that the period of youth is a period when one is full of vitality and the will to fight, and a time when one increases his knowledge and grows up: it is a time when one should dedicate himself to the Communist enterprise, diligently study Mao Tse-tung's thought, relentlessly repudiate the old world, and commit himself to the fiery three great revolutionary movements to weather the storm, see the world and be tempered into steel-like hardness. Getting married too early will not only weaken our revolutionary will, but will also impose financial burdens on us. Therefore, we suggest that responsible comrades at all levels, and the organization of the Communist Youth League and the Red Guards, should continue to educate the young people to persist in late marriage, and apply their energy to the cause of socialist revolution and socialist construction.

COURTSHIP PROBLEMS

There are reasons why courtship can be difficult in a missionary setting and this needs to be appreciated. Within a small limited group, a man probably becomes interested in the most eligible attractive female in the group. In a larger circle he might not look at her or be especially attracted. It has to be faced that the field of choice is much smaller once someone has gone abroad, and there may only be two or three eligible girls around. The chosen girl may be of a different nationality, and there are real practical problems in cross-cultural marriages. Neither partner knows the other's parents, nor are they familiar with the cultural mores or the home church situation of the other. Each of them tends to feel isolated and alienated in the other's culture on furlough. Moreover, after a few years a decision will have to be made regarding which is to be the homeland of the children, and in which they are to be educated. This then means seeing less and less of the parents of the other partner. The practical problems have to be faced.

But the small choice presents another problem. A girl may feel that she was chosen only because the field of choice was so small, and have an inferiority complex about it which can put a strain on the marriage later. While most missionary marriages are happy, it is observable that sometimes they are not, and one wonders whether in other circumstances such people would have married at all. All in all, then, it seems better to make one's choice from the widest available field in one's own home country. There are of course very many happy mission-field marriages, many of them intranational, but courtship is difficult in the rather restricted society overseas.

A young male missionary may meet the problem of how to make his first approach. If he is dead certain already, head over heels in love, etc., then there is little problem. But suppose he is more cautious. He wants an opportunity to try to get to know a young girl missionary better, and invites her out for coffee, or takes her out for a walk. In the small restricted circle the girl's hopes are bound to be raised, and in all probability other girls will notice and there will be speculation and gossip on their part. How is he to get to know her better without raising her hopes and causing others to tease and drop hints? I have known of young missionaries who have courted two or three girls, and have been engaged to two or three. It scarcely helps, particularly if they have to go on meeting for years. It is cruel to raise hopes which are then dashed. Even where the young eligible bachelor missionary is scrupulously careful, there may be several girls who openly, or secretly, hope that he may develop an interest in their direction. I have even met girls who declared that they had been led to verses of Scripture and in other ways had received specific guidance from the Lord, and yet the fellow concerned had not the slightest interest in them.

Enough has been said on this sensitive subject to show something of the problems that exist. There are still others that arise from the nature of the cultures in the country concerned. It seems improper in some countries for young unmarried people to be seen around together or for them to stay in the same house. In others it would not cause comment normally; but if they were engaged or known to be interested in each other, then it would be thought most improper for them to be under the same roof for a night. All manner of complicated arrangements for staying in different homes in the same city, making opportunities for meeting each other without the others present, etc., have to be made, and this can take away something of the joyful spontaneity which should characterize courtship.

CHILDREN

Those in full-time Christian service are unlikely to have much treasure on earth. We are all told to be content with necessities (1 Ti 6:8), but children are treasure indeed. The joy of being able to hold your own baby in your arms, to help a toddler walk, to see the first joy of reading, to wrestle with small son or tomboy daughter, to see them growing up and becoming more of a companion, more adult, to share with one's life partner in helping one's own children in all the realities of life: this is treasure, earthly pleasure beyond all other, in God-given human relationships. The family relationship is the most highly esteemed in many cultures, and no less so in the Bible. This relationship, above all others, mirrors, although feebly, our relationship with God and with fellow Christians in the church.

But, remember, there is cost here also. For inevitably the best interests of our children may mean separation. Where missionaries live in large city centers suitable schooling may be available: American schools, British army schools, and even in some places Christian schools. But for those in more pioneer situations this is not possible.

One quickly learns how bored a child can be at home when not fully occupied, especially once his mind is active enough to want to learn. Some parents try to educate their children at home, and sometimes there is no alternative. But a child needs the company and competition of his peers (as well as the love of his parents). Generally, however, if a child is to learn to read and write his own language, and to be educated in his own culture, it becomes necessary for him to go to some suitable primary school. In more rugged missionary situations this may mean a small mission-organized, primary-age boarding school away from home. (It is not like a secular boarding school in that usually all the other children and all the teachers are already known as friends and honorary "aunts.") Undeniably it costs the parents more than it does the children. The children are initially homesick, but after that the passage of time moves on more easily. Parents feel the loss more heavily.

The children would doubtless feel it more, were it not that all the other children face the same problems, and leaving home for school is the accepted thing in the small limited circle in which they live.[4]

Our own personal experience has been that our relationship with our children has been deepened because of separations; we value our time together all the more, and appreciate one another all the more. At first, children's letters are not always very satisfactory, but letters from teachers and houseparents can help to bridge the gap.

But now comes the harder decision still. In their sensitive teen years, what is the best thing to do? There are various possibilities. First, in some countries it is possible for children to attend national schools. From a purely theoretical point of view this would be the ideal identification. But several problems arise:

1. The country concerned may not really accept foreign children, who thus can suffer from a sense of alienation. Few countries recognize aliens and accord them full citizenship, even when they are born and brought up in their country. Color prejudice acts in all directions. The tolerance accorded to foreign children may diminish as they get older.

2. Growing children become less and less able to take their place in their own home country. For example, they may not be able to pass the necessary qualifying examinations for higher education or the career of their choice. True, they probably have a first-rate knowledge of a foreign language. But by fol-

[4]"If a child is born into an environment where it is the normal and accepted thing for him to go away to school, and if parents have really and truly accepted this as the normal way, there is, except in cases of children with some personality defect, very little difficulty. Going to boarding school is just another thing to look forward to. When you are so many years old, you will have a bicycle of your own; and when you are so many years old you will be able to take the exam for a driver's licence" (letter quoted in J. R. Beck, *Parental Preparation of Missionary Children for Boarding School*, published by the Committee to Assist Missionary Education Overseas (CAMEO).

lowing such a course, while they may have a reasonable hope
(if academically minded enough) of becoming university professors in the adopted language or even of becoming their
home country's ambassador, many children may resent being so
circumscribed, feeling that they have not had a fair deal educationally as far as settling down in their own national culture is concerned. It is also unlikely that the foster culture
will really accept them fully.

3. In these days of moral decline in missionary-sending
countries, it is no longer necessarily true to talk of the great
moral dangers to which a teenager is exposed in a more per-
missive society, where the major sins are social rather than
sexual. Nonetheless, the far greater problems of cross-cultural
and interracial marriage have to be faced if your teenaged son
or daughter is to grow up among attractive members of another
race. It is not a matter of thinking in a vacuum how desirable
such a marriage might be ethnically from a purely biological
standpoint. Even in those cities where Eurasian children are
more readily accepted, there still remain strong prejudices
against "mixed" marriages. Singapore is probably one of the
most integrated and tolerant multiracial societies in Asia, and
yet Chinese and Tamils alike have strong prejudices against
their children marrying those of other races. I remember my
own surprise at the strength of this prejudice in a discussion
about marriage between Caucasian and Asian missionary leaders. The Asians were unanimously against it, but suggested
that if Caucasians opposed it they would be accused of racial
prejudice. "Let *us* discourage the young people," they said!
This is not to say that there may not be exceptions, but the
problems must be realistically faced.

Second, some have tried to educate their own children on
the field. If the parents are teachers, it is not impossible at the
primary level, though a child misses his peers. At a secondary
level it is all but impossible. We once escorted home two such

teenagers, who seemed almost illiterate in their own country's literature.

Third, it is possible for parents to return home with their children. If, as sometimes happens, this fits in conveniently with a missionary society's need for some reasonably young representation in the sending country, they can perhaps stay at home for seven or eight years and see their children through the teen years. The greater the spread of the family, the longer this will take, of course. There can never be blanket recommendations about such things. Families differ, even children within a family differ; and the needs of the individual must be respected. Nonetheless, sometimes one wonders if some parents' return was not governed more by a reluctance on their part to let their children stand on their own feet.

Fourth, in some centers there are field schools available at the secondary level though these are sometimes extremely expensive to run as private schools. I have already mentioned the American friend of mine with six children at one time all attending a Christian private school in Japan, who needed to raise an enormous sum to educate them. Few single home churches would be prepared to budget quite so much for the support of one missionary couple and their children.

The fifth alternative is to make arrangements at home with small family-size hostels run by missionary societies, so that the children may either attend local day schools or, in some countries, boarding schools (where all the children are separated from their families and thus there is more equality of environment). This means longer separation from parents although, with today's cheaper charter flights, missionary children, like the children of military or business people, are more able to come out for prolonged summer vacation visits to join their parents living abroad. This approach, while it deprives children of their parents' constant attention during the teen years, does enable them to grow up in their own home country and to be fully accepted and adapted to it.

The relative merits and deficiencies of these approaches must be weighed against each other. They may, and do, vary from family to family and child to child. Personally I do not believe that the number of problem children among those who are so deprived of their parents' presence (not of their love and constant communication by means of letter, letter-tape, etc.) is any greater than among those who grow up at home and face battles and generation-gap problems with their all-too-present parents.

Few of us who have to face such separations regard them as ideal. Naturally we wish they could be avoided. But the missionary has set his hand to the plow; his third and fourth terms of service (the second decade of service) are probably the most fruitful. The language is well understood, experience of the culture has been gained, and to return home at that stage is to waste training and experience. After a ten-year gap, energies are beginning to diminish and often a language has almost to be relearned. If they are to take seriously the call to sacrificial discipleship, this is part of the cost to be paid by the parents who love, miss, and yearn over their children, and pore anxiously and prayerfully over every letter as it comes.

There are some insensitive people with an overdose of psychological theory who have apparently forgotten what the Bible has to say about the secondary position even of family loyalties in true discipleship,[5] who speak out about sacrificing Jephthah's daughter and offering children to Molech. Such implied criticism inflicts grievous wounds on those for whom discipleship has demanded this costly course.

[5]See, e.g., Lk 14:26: "If any one comes to me and does not hate his own father and mother and wife and children and brothers and sisters, yes, and even his own life, he cannot be my disciple."

Size of Families

The illustration above of the missionary with six children probably raised some queries in your mind. How big a family should a misionary have? I would suggest no bigger than they would have had if they had remained at home. On a home wage and salary there are limits to the size of family that people can afford. It seems quite wrong to raise a larger family than one would have had otherwise on the generous and sacrificial giving of the church. The wife in any case is tied down by bearing and bringing up small children, and has less time to help in active evangelism and church-planting.

In a missionary society which gives increased allowances for children and provides for their education, every additional child means less for the single missionaries and the married without children. Little will be said, but in days of financial shortness this is a factor which considerate people will not forget.

Increasingly in the world at large the problem of over-population is being tackled by Africasian countries through encouraging birth control. In places like Japan and Singapore, where two or three children are now considered the patriotic norm for the responsible citizen, it seems strange if the missionary shows little evidence of any similar sense of responsibility. Few missionary societies have been prepared to make rules about limiting families, though some have refused to give allowances for children beyond a certain number, or have a fixed salary which is not increased with the size of the family (as happens in most secular situations in the home countries). But the increasingly strong pressure for family planning in the countries to which missionaries go demands that the matter of the size of the family be realistically considered as part of the Christians' witness and testimony in countries where limitation is expected.

ADOPTION

What attitude should missionaries take to adoption? If a couple is childless, then should they not be allowed to adopt children? It is quite striking how such a procedure then encourages the birth of a child by normal means! Again, if there is an only child and no prospect of a second, why not adopt a second child as company for the first?

There are increased pressures to adopt also the many unwanted or orphan children often badly provided for in developing countries. Because there are mixed-blood children resulting from the immoral behavior of foreign troops, and because these children are discriminated against, there would seem often to be an increased responsibility to adopt unwanted children rather than having more children of one's own.

But there are certain questions to be asked:

1. Are missionaries able to give such children the kind of stable homelife which they require? Adopted children face greater problems than natural ones as it is. Because of the nature of their calling, the need for separation, the problems of education and so on, as outlined above, missionaries do not seem the best qualified to provide the kind of permanent home which a potentially disturbed child may require.

2. Is it the aim of the sending church that its missionaries, to whom Providence has afforded no children, should then take on (at the expense of the sending churches) the cost of supporting other children? Biological methods of growing a family at least have some limits afforded by the length of gestation and the physical strength of the mother. There are no limits to the number of children which could be adopted! If there is a definite policy of founding orphanages, there would be no objection. But it does need to be realized that missionaries should not take advantage of their mode of support to do what they might not be able to do on a fixed salary in a secular occupation.

3. The chief aim of the missionary is church-planting. He has joined a group with a limited and definite aim. Adopting large families may be a distraction from the main aim, unless there is clear guidance to the contrary.

There was actually a most interesting case of adoption from the early history of the Christian church in Thailand, or Siam as it was then. The first missionaries labored for nineteen years without a convert, and then the first convert was a Chinese and not a Thai. The country was unhealthy for everybody and the annual death toll from malaria ran into scores of thousands. Of the early missionaries, no less than sixty-one died in action. But one couple adopted a Thai child and educated her. She became a Christian and at the time of her death was survived by more than one hundred descendants, all of whom claimed to be (at least nominally) Christian.[6] In a highly resistant culture perhaps that was the only way. But generally the legal complications of adopting a national child are formidable.

LATER LIFE

The sacrifice of the missionary does not stop in later life. As they get older, they miss their children and their grandchildren. They cannot afford as a rule to fly home for every wedding and be around to watch over each grandchild's birth. There is a cost for the married as well as the unmarried. How glorious are the reunions! How wonderful are those opportunities, when they come, for the missionary grandparents to come home and see the mature children and delight in their grandchildren! But some of that enjoyment can come only through correspondence and photographs. The best education of children may be incompatible with maximum family proximity, but maximum family *unity* can be maintained even

[6]Kenneth Wells, *History of Protestant Work in Thailand* (Bangkok: Church of Christ in Thailand, 1958).

when separated. Families which live together are not always united. Families which are forced to live apart can often have a most precious unity. Make that your aim and prayer.

RESPONSIBILITY TO ONE'S PARENTS

It would be appropriate here to take a look at the missionary's responsibility to his or her own parents. When James and John were called by the Lord, "they left their father Zebedee in the boat with the hired servants, and went away to follow Him" (Mk 1:20, NASB). Later their mother appears, asking that her two sons might have leading places in the kingdom of Christ (Mt 20:20-21). This reminds us that, whatever the sacrifices some missionaries may still have to make, frequently missionaries' parents make even greater ones. So often their delight is in their children and grandchildren, and when they see them departing to a foreign country for an anticipated four or five years, they naturally wonder whether they will ever see them again. The cost and the sacrifice of elderly parents of missionaries is great, and we should honor those who, like Zebedee, are left behind to carry on the business without the help and comfort of their children.

Some parents are thoroughly sympathetic with their children's missionary work and are a wonderful help to them through their prayers, and their personal ministry in lovingly prepared packages, regular cheerful letters, etc. They want their children to be successful in their vocation, as did Zebedee's wife. Other parents are hostile, unsympathetic, and resentful of their children's absence, failing to understand how they can be willing to leave their parents and homeland behind for some distant and presumably barbarous place. (Although in these more affluent days the possibility of missionaries' parents visiting their children overseas can help to alter a lot of unfavorable attitudes and misconceptions.) But whether parents are sympathetic or antagonistic, our Christian re-

sponsibilty to them remains the same even if it is more difficult
to exercise.

Sometimes Jesus' statement in Luke 14:26, "If any one comes
to Me, and does not hate his own father and mother and wife
and children and brothers and sisters, yes, and even his own
life, he cannot be My disciple" (NASB), is quoted as though
that were the simple answer to responsibility toward parents.
This is a gross oversimplification. Elsewhere the Christian husband is commanded to love his wife "as Christ also loved the
church" (Eph 5:25). One could scarcely use Christ's words to
justify a man separating from his wife in order to preach the
gospel overseas. When, as happens not at all infrequently, one
of our missionaries faces the possibility of returning home to
care for an ailing mother or father, I never feel free to quote
this verse, for I feel it refers to becoming a disciple and is relevant in situations where an individual's closest relatives may
seek to prevent him from becoming a disciple of Christ at all.
Rather, I endeavor to point out that loving and serving one's
parents is just as much a part of being a Christian as making
disciples of all nations. Obedience to the command of Christ
means not only leaving one's own land and parents in order to
preach the gospel, but also returning to one's own land to obey
the commandment, "Honour thy father and thy mother."

There should be no conflict of loyalties in this situation.
Christ speaks severely to those who neglect the clear command
of God about responsibility to support one's parents on the alleged grounds that they have higher spiritual responsibilites
(Mk 7:12-13). Paul speaks equally strongly: "If any one does
not provide for his relatives, and especially for his own family,
he has disowned the faith and is worse than an unbeliever"
(1 Ti 5:8, RSV). It does not seem possible for a Christian to
say, "I cannot come home to help, because I have a higher call."
It must be recognized that sometimes married brothers and
sisters who are unwilling to accept the responsibility them-

selves may strongly pressure an unmarried missionary sister, feeling that she is the one who can most easily pull up her roots in order to help their parents. Where the missionary is the only available relative, his or her responsibility is much clearer. It is more difficult when the compelling factor is the selfishness of other relatives who are capable but unwilling to care for their own parents. Here again, though, the Christian is surely one who gladly responds to demonstrate love and affection in willingly accepting responsibility.

There may be times when comparatively youthful parents in good health and well provided for with other children to comfort them still bring pressure to prevent a young person going as a missionary at all. In this situation Luke 9:59-62 *would* seem to be relevant, and the heart must be steeled to bid an affectionate farewell in spite of opposition. But when parents are old and weak and needing care which no one else can give, then, in my judgment, however zealous the missionary may be, he or she is normally bound to return home to fulfill his or her responsibilities, and to do it joyfully and cheerfully without any sense of frustration or conflict of loyalties. Later, when the closing years of the parents have been filled with sunshine, the way may then open again for the Christian to resume overseas service. The way of obedience is not always easy, but its excellence and wholesomeness are plain.

In many Asian countries, if it were known that a missionary had aged parents at home, improperly cared for, it would inflict lasting damage on that missionary's reputation as a Christian and on his integrity as a human being.

CONCLUSION

Missionaries are sexual beings. They are not clothed with asbestos, nor immune to those temptations which are common to man and to woman. They are sexually tempted daily just like everyone else, perhaps more so because the adversary es-

pecially aims his fiery darts at those who are in the forefront
of the church's leadership. Moral failure always seems to be
news, and the failure of Christians who profess a higher ethic
is always seized upon by the enemies of the gospel.

The happiest answer to this problem—to put it at its lowest,
as the Book of Common Prayer (following 1 Co 7:9) used to—
is the happily married couple. Marriage relationships, happy
physically and emotionally, are more than ever important
where a couple may be isolated from other social contacts with
fellow countrymen and where they must provide a pattern to
newly converted pagans of what a Christian homelife is like.
In the busyness and tiredness of a missionary life, real communication between husband and wife is more than ever important. The foundations of such a relationship will be laid
in many cases before departing for service overseas. The sta-
bility and depth of the relationship is one test of suitability for
such service.

For others the way is harder. They may certainly be sent
"two and two," for this is a biblical pattern for working, although it must be admitted that certain hardy spirits seem to
work better on their own! Although their calling is to be unmarried, the Lord has promised that "everyone who has left
houses or brothers or sisters or father or mother or children or
farms, for My name's sake, shall receive as many times as much,
and shall inherit eternal life" (Mt 19:29, NASB). My experience is that this promise is one that He delights to keep. Within the "household of faith" we can especially minister to one
another the blessings that we may have thought we had for-
feited.

7 Cultures, Communication, and Identification

PAUL MAKES IT CLEAR that, in his attitude to Jews, to Greeks, to those within and without the law, to the weak, he sought to "become as a Jew," etc., in order to win them (1 Co 9:20 ff.). In other words, within a number of different cultures existing contemporaneously, the Christian missionary has to make a deliberate, conscious, and sustained effort to live and work and think and speak in the framework of that culture. It is my own conviction, also, that this same principle holds for cultures which succeed each other chronologically and that, as Christians, we need to make vigorous efforts in changing cultures to adapt ourselves to presenting the unchanging gospel in terms of the changing environment. One questions the necessity of using seventeenth-century language, eighteenth-century hymns, and nineteenth-century evangelistic methods to reach twentieth-century man. It is strange that people who see this within their own country are slow to appreciate how different other cultures are.

And cultures are certainly different! The experience of a Japanese friend of mine who was invited out to dinner in North America serves as a good illustration. It would obviously be discourteous, he thought, to arrive at the time specified, as in all probability they might not be ready, and so he arrived half an hour late. His hostess seemed pleased to see him (as well she might, having held dinner warming in the oven for the past half hour, but it might not be ruined yet), and his courteous host asked him if he would like to "use the bathroom," a form of euphemism commonly understood in the

Western world. The visitor disappeared, the door was locked, and soon the sound of running bath water caused consternation in the kitchen. Almost an hour later, a happy, glowing Japanese emerged to meet his glowering hosts. He was delighted because they were the nicest Americans he had ever met, who showed a proper hospitality and understanding of Japanese culture. In a Japanese hotel a bath is always taken before dinner, like a course before the soup, and to offer a guest the use of your domestic bath is a special courtesy much appreciated. Unfortunately the Americans were unaware of the very favorable impression they had created, and were seething at this discourteous foreigner who, having already arrived half an hour late, then proceeded to stew in the bath (of all the unheard-of things) for a further hour!

This, you will agree, is a glorious example of cross-cultural misunderstanding! The fantastic thing is that some people find it very hard to make the necessary adjustments. They assume that, if they behave as they would in their own country, everyone will understand.[1]

THE NEED FOR ADAPTATION

A famous English preacher once caused an uproar in the south of Ireland when, in preaching against worldliness, he spoke of "girls with lips the color of letterboxes." Though they might be red in his own country, in independent Eire letterboxes are a brilliant emerald green!

A basic three-point gospel, assuming some understanding of the use of the word *God* as a proper name, may not be understood in a culture where it is a common noun used to describe a whole class of objects. John 3:16 is deservedly a favorite text in English-speaking countries where, with a long background of Christendom, "eternal life" is regarded as something worth possessing. In some other contexts it may cause some

[1]See also E. Nida, *Customs, Culture and Christianity* (New York: Harper, 1954).

confusion. In a Hindu culture, for example, it is assumed that everyone has eternal life already, and is fated to be reborn over and over again. The great desire is to come to the end of that endless wheel of karma and to be rid of eternal life. Therefore, while eternal life and being born again may be good ways to speak of the gospel in some cultures, they may be very confusing ways of speaking in another.

In recent years there has been a vogue for mass evangelism in which people are urged to make "a decision," involving an appeal to come forward at the end in order to be counseled and perhaps to receive an instruction booklet. In the Western context, embarrassment and shyness make it quite a costly thing for people to come forward, and coming forward thus becomes a real test of sincerity and desire to find Christ. But even in a Western context there is still a danger of spurious conversion, of people going forward without really knowing why. In some Asian contexts, however, this approach may be almost disastrous. There are factors which encourage people to go forward. Politeness is one, because after the evangelists and others have so kindly presented this rather long entertainment, complete with soloists, marimbas, choirs, and the rest, it would be discourteous to opt out of what is apparently the intended climax of the meeting. Good manners demand that one should go forward.[2] Curiosity too, for after all, what happens to those people who go forward? And how kind to provide a free gift booklet; it would be good to receive one. The making of a momentary decision, if that is what is required, can mean very little. Yet, in the Japanese context there is a deeply ingrained concept of (extremely feudal) loyalty to a lord which is lifelong, and unto death. Japanese history and literature glorifies such a concept of loyalty. A call, therefore, to become a lifelong retainer of Jesus Christ is a tremendous

[2]At one such large meeting a Christian who had brought a non-Christian turned in perplexity to me and said, "She wants to know if it is all right if she doesn't go forward"!

decision, not to be compared with the decision to go down to the front to discover what the culmination of the meeting might be!

WAYS OF MAKING FRIENDS

It is so easy for us to bring with us entirely foreign concepts of informality and hospitality and making friends. There is the amusing story of the Western businessman in Japan who invited his national employees to his home for what in his own culture is known as a wiener roast (in England as a sausage sizzle). In the American context, the wiener roast appears to be a cultic ceremony harking back to the good old pioneering days of the covered wagon and cooking on open fires under the stars. It is a particularly pleasant and informal way of putting off one's dignity and getting to meet people. But imagine the embarrassment and puzzlement of his Japanese employees when, invited to this pleasant home with its lovely kitchen, they found themselves shown into the garden where their boss was wearing an apron, handing out half-burned wieners smoked on an open fire. Were they not worthy of a decent meal inside the house? And why on earth should the boss do his own cooking in this undignified manner? He was trying, of course, to make friends in terms of his own culture rather than theirs.

We had a similar experience once when we invited some Japanese neighbors to a meal with us. It was to be a Japanese meal with chopsticks, of course; we knew that much. The wife was a Christian who went out to work in order to support her children because her husband, who had lost his job in unfortunate circumstances, was out of work. We knew that they were often hungry. What better way was there than to invite them in and give them a good meal, and thus get to know the husband as well in order that he might come to faith in Christ also?

On Wednesday evening we waited in vain, long past the expected time, and finally ate alone, crestfallen and puzzled. Later that evening when they returned home and apologized at having had other business, we should have taken the hint. But Christians are persistent people. "Well, come on Friday. And please don't forget on Friday; we shall be waiting for you." On Friday the man came alone, wearing his most formal kimono and bringing an expensive present of two bottles of concentrated fruit punch. It was an awkward occasion with long silences.

At last it began to dawn that we were doing the wrong thing. Because we were the teachers of his wife they were already in our debt. And now we insisted on their eating with us, putting them in our debt still further. They felt that they could not reciprocate our hospitality by taking us out for a meal, and still less could they invite us to their unworthy home, where the wife would not eat with us, but serve us. Therefore a gift must be brought in order to repay the obligation, and the value of the gift was several times the cost of the meal. Instead of helping them, we had further impoverished them. Instead of making friends, we had created an awkwardness and embarrassment that even now makes us blush to remember.

Quite apart from bowing, or bringing up one's hands in a *nemasti,* avoiding using the left hand (used for toilet purposes), avoiding touching the head, avoiding pointing the feet, not drinking all the juice in the glass, making the appropriately appreciative food noises and so on, there is a great deal to learn in adapting to different cultures. Being indirect, dropping and picking up hints, never contradicting someone or making him lose face: all this must be learned, and our crude Western directness unlearned. Committee meetings take longer too, and the way of reaching a consensus (or a stalemate) more prolonged in order to avoid any direct showdown.

THINKING CROSS-CULTURALLY

It is not enough to adapt your behavior and your speaking. If at all possible you want to learn to *think* in the way of the people with whom you are living. This is very hard. In order to do so you will have to try to understand the whole historical, religious, and philosophical environment and thought patterns of those to whom you go. Why are Japanese such dreadful liars? Are they? When someone asks us a question, we try to answer it. We are not especially subtle and think on the surface. But when a Japanese, for example, hears a question he looks behind the question. What lies behind it? Why does this man ask it? What kind of an answer does he want to hear? So that the reply you get may not be what we call "the truth," but rather the answer that he thinks you want to hear.

This can be very frustrating, of course. I ask a plumber to come and repair a broken water pipe. He knows that he is too busy to do so for a whole week. But to refuse might make me angry, or might make me take my business elsewhere. "Will you come tomorrow?" "Yes." But tomorrow he does not come. I wait until the very last moment tomorrow before realizing that he is not coming. I have been kept happy for twenty-four hours. The next morning (thirty-six hours) I call him. "Why didn't you come yesterday?" "I am very sorry. Some unavoidable business arose. I am sorry." "Can you come today?" "Yes, I will come tomorrow." Tomorrow dawns (sixty hours) and I wait until nightfall. By this time (seventy-two hours) it is too late to do anything until the next morning (eighty-four hours). Then, very angry, I decide that I will go and see him. I arrive and meet his wife. He is unaccountably missing, but will be back any moment. The moment drags on. I suspect that he will not return while I am there. I am right. I go home crestfallen, having left a message with the wife that he must come as soon as possible. But now it is the weekend and perhaps he cannot come— Soon a whole week has passed and at last he arrives, very apologetic about it all.

Why could he not have explained to begin with? Because for centuries in the culture of Japan the *samurai* class carried swords and had the right to cut down any farmer, artisan, or merchant (who carried no swords). Naturally you bowed to the inevitable and always gave the answer which would please, and such careful avoidance of offense is now deeply ingrained.

But associated with this is also the sense of the unreality of life. To the Buddhist there is no tomorrow. Compare, for example, what the dictionary will give as equivalent expressions for use on parting: *Sayonara* equals "good-bye." Good-bye is a thoroughly Christian concept, based on a pluralist philosophy: there is a God and there is a you and this God will be with you to do something for you. To the Buddhist, a monist, there is no separate god; all things are all part of the one pantheistic totality. There is no you. As an idealist he sees you only as a figment in his imagination. *Sayonara* is a thoroughly fatalistic concept, meaning literally, "If that's the way it is [that's the way it's gonna be!]." We have had the illusion of meeting, and now we have the illusion of parting. It's all very sad and tragic, but there is nothing to be done about it. We have enjoyed meeting them in the same way as we meet figures on the television screen. They have intrigued us, we should have liked to have known them better, but now it seems the play is over, and the insubstantial image on the television of my sense organs fades away: "If that's the way it is."

Such a fatalistic view, of course, strikes at the roots of all morality. What happens is what happens; it is all very sad, but there is nothing to be done about it. The concept of responsibility for sin is consequently absent in a monistic system. Traditional Christian arguments sound rather silly: "I think, therefore I am" is a useful concept where the thinker accepts a realistic philosophy. But to the idealist thinker you must retranslate it as "I have the illusion of thinking and so I have the illusion of being"—and where does that get you?

COMMUNICATION IN EVANGELISM

All this may seem very nebulous. But you see how foolish it is to translate your Western words, to make your Western assumptions, and preach your Western gospel? Someone recently wrote an article entitled "I did not mean what you thought I said I meant," and this is the great problem of communication. I must first understand what my hearer understands. I may use certain words and intend to inject into them a certain meaning. But this is useless if that meaning is not in fact communicated at all. I may say, or mean to say, "God hates the sins of men"; but my hearer may get the message, "god (s) hate human crime." I mean a proper name, the one true God, Creator of heaven and earth. They hear an indefinite common noun of uncertain number. Because there is no concept of responsibility, it means that a perverse and remorseless fate is determined to deal with me because of the crimes which I have unfortunately been caused to commit.

Perhaps enough has been said to show that it takes time to understand another culture and to communicate the gospel in terms which will not be misundertsood. The current view that a couple of years of one's life donated to missionary service is probably sufficient ignores this whole question of cross-cultural communication. The gospel is a stone to be thrown, a book or tract to be given; the hearers are responsible for what they hear. But are they, if you have made no effort really to communicate, and they have not understood what they have heard? There is the tragically comic notion that missionary evangelism is raiding a village, giving everyone in it a tract, blaring some memorized phrases through a loudspeaker, and then going down to one's house, justified that one has preached the gospel. It is now up to the hearers to respond. It would be cheaper to use a tape recorder or pay distributors. This pitifully simplistic view of missionary work is hopeless. People are regarded as "resistant" to the gospel when it may never have been communicated clearly and meaningfully to them at all. But it must be, as this is what Christ has commanded us to do.

LIVING

How do we live? Do we take with us all that we take if we were settling in our own land: all our labor-saving devices, our large private car, our Western beds, and our modes of living? Standards vary from country to country, of course, and increasingly many of the things we take for granted are becoming fairly common in cities in some more advanced "mission fields." But at what level am I going to live? That of the local rich man? Or of the local poor man? If I live at either extreme my social contacts with the other extreme will probably be minimal. So I will probably settle for whatever is intermediate in that particular community. That intermediate standard will vary according to whether I am stationed in a city, provincial town, or a tribal village. Great adaptability is necessary. In the city I will need a vehicle to get around just as the nationals do. In a tribal situation there are probably no roads. In a provincial situation a vehicle may be useful for trips to other outlying places, but locally I will get to know more people, and more people will get to know me, if I walk or bicycle, so that there may be smiles and greetings, bows and conversations.

Even today you will hear criticisms of missionaries because of their standards of living. "They live in the wealthiest parts of town. The only views of Chinese they hear are those of their employees," said a Cantonese-speaking Christian leader to me the other day. An intelligent student from Indonesia wrote recently to a missionary:

> Are they *truly* sent by the Lord to go to Indonesia? Or are they only very expert in writing in their missionary maga-

zines that so many souls have been won for Christ . . . or that in their region many people are hungry for the Word of the Lord, *etc., etc.?* I am very happy when I see true servants of the Lord, used of God. But my disappointment mounts when I see people who come such a long way from the West [missionaries] who are *not* good witnesses, specially in their lives, when they cannot adjust to us. . . .

The first problem is that of physical adjustment to the native environment both in the home and in the general manner of life. A missionary is called to cross national and cultural barriers which separate peoples of this world. He is the apostle to the Gentiles, a calling which necessitates a break with his own people and the adoption of a new home in a strange land. But as far as I see, they make no effort to adapt to the ways of a foreign country, as we would expect a guest to adjust his life in the home of a friend. I only write this because of my disappointment. . . .[3]

The pattern of a Christ who identified Himself with men, and the approach of Paul of being "all things to all men" suggest that we should go as far as we can go to shed unnecessary cultural differences, without being ridiculous or endangering health. In a modern Asian city, where most businessmen wear Western-style suits, it would be absurd for the missionary to affect national dress. In a tribal or village situation, it might not seem out of place. If small houses are normal and nationals sleep on the Korean *ondol* (hot-floor) , or Japanese *tatami,* or on tribal bamboo, it is acceptable for missionaries to do the same. Such houses have no room for separate "bedrooms" in any case. Soft and comfortable down mattresses may be stored in the wall cupboards. Your visitor feels most at home kneeling on the floor; he knows which is the humble side of the room: he knows how to drink green tea from a small bowl. To make a country peasant keep his shoes on, sit on a chair, balance a cup and saucer, spoon and sandwich like a juggler in a circus is to make him feel thoroughly off balance. To adapt to the pat-

---

[3]From a private letter, part in Indonesian and part in English.

tern with which he is familiar is the best way to put him at his ease.

Societies differ. In a more sophisticated city, your Western way of living may be an attraction. But generally considerable adaptation is advisable. Otherwise your missionary is like a spaceman coming out of his hermetically sealed alien capsule.

LEARNING A LANGUAGE

Generally speaking it is unwise to try to learn a foreign language except in the environment in which it is spoken. In general, too, it is unwise to try to study by yourself. The spoken language is primary; unless one knows the really authentic sounds it is asking for trouble to start reading symbols representing those sounds before you know the correct sounds. It is much harder to correct a mistaken pronunciation once it is habitual than it is to form a new habit. Unless the foreign language can be studied under the supervision of a national of that country (not some alien who happens to speak it "after a fashion"), with plenty of opportunity to listen to the language being spoken or to listen to properly prepared tapes or records with supervision, it is far better to wait until you are in a situation where a language may be heard all day long. You will not understand very much that you hear, but at least the correct sounds, rhythm, intonations, and mode of speaking (at the back of the throat or all tangled up with the teeth, etc.) will become fixed in your brain and you can imitate them and start to make sounds yourself before you face any written symbols.

When you get to your field of work, remember that learning the language is basic to your future usefulness. Pressures will be brought upon you to start doing this and that. You yourself will be eager to start preaching. But remember that there is little point in preaching your heart out if it does not get into the heart of the other fellow. You can make noises, and use

words, but if the net result is incomprehensibility, you have
made no contribution to that person's salvation, however much
satisfaction you may kid yourself you are getting. J. K. Stephen
wrote,

> Two voices are there: one is of the deep;
> And one is of an old half-witted sheep,
> Which bleats articulate monotony,
> And Wordsworth, both are thine.

But if your language is inadequate, please read "*in*articulate
monotony"; and if you have not taken seriously the need to
understand the country and its patterns of thought, read "ir-
relevant, inarticulate monotony." And who wants to be that
kind of missionary? In those early months nothing matters
like language-learning. This is the foundation of your whole
ministry. People may get converted through people using inadequate language, broken speech, and baby words like "got"
and "put." I was so converted myself. But few people want to
remain having to listen regularly to totally inadequate vocabulary. It is possible to memorize a simple explanation of the
meaning of the cross, but this scarcely exhausts the riches of its
meaning, and no one wants to hear those same four phrases
again and again without elaboration and development.

Language-learning is intriguing at first. But then comes the
hard upward climb when you wonder if you are making any
progress at all. The temptation is to give up. Good long
chunks of consecutive study are essential. Occasional short opportunities usually mean that one does little more than revise
what one has forgotten from last time. It is possible to get
along with very little. But few people who do that become
effective evangelists and still fewer become effective teachers.
Give language everything you have got.

A LIFELONG HABIT OF STUDY

It is tragic to find missionaries who have learned nothing

new for years. The good missionary is always learning new words and new phrases. He is a lifelong learner. He is always exploring the country's literature, history, and tradition to find new ways of expressing biblical truth. I still remember my delight in discovering the Japanese concept of "honorable departure." Still more I remember the response of a far from sophisticated congregation when I told them, "In the Kabuki play, *The Generalissimo leaves Edo* [you could see them all sit up] after the Generalissimo has been persuaded to abdicate in the first act; in the second the curtain rises at dawn at the bridge on the outskirts of Tokyo. . . . Now the Generalissimo enters with his retainers and everybody grovels before him. The *samisens* are twanging and the commentator explains that, after several hundred years of rule by a succession of Generalissimos, at last *the most honorable foot* is about to step out of the capital. You cannot miss the most honorable feet; they are wearing huge boots. The Generalissimo makes his final speech and then comes this tremendous dramatic moment, when he turns to the bridge, and everybody holds their breath; and then the most honorable foot stretches out and down. . . . It is a tremendous moment of emotion at his departure, and the whole crowd bursts out sobbing! This is 'honorable departure.' Now in Matthew 28:19 the most honorable foot, after thirty-three years in this world, is about to step out of it. What will he say at this moment of 'honorable parting'? What are the last words that he leaves with them? 'Go and make disciples of all nations. . . .' "

No wonder this left such an indelible impression on them. Do you see how an understanding and local illustration of this kind lends tremendous force to preaching? To gain increasing understanding of such matters—of the sports, the plays, the stories, as well as contemporary government reports—is not something which will be grasped in a short two- or three-year "tourist missionary term." It takes a lifetime of understanding and continued application in order to be able to get truth across.

Though the next chapter discusses the nonprofessional missionary, it needs to be considered against this background of the need for deep cultural understanding. Few nonprofessionals (except in places where English is the language of education) , especially if they only give four or five years, are able to penetrate very deeply into a culture which requires such application. It should be stressed also that, while some cultures are monolithic and one language is sufficient, others demand that the missionary master two or three languages in order to converse at any depth with the various people he meets. A smattering of a trade language may be sufficient for trade; it is rarely enough for effective communication.

8 Professional or Nonprofessional?

As INDICATED EARLIER, it all depends upon what you mean by "missionary." If every Christian is a missionary then the word means very little. If by "missionary" one means specifically a person who is sent by the churches for the work of evangelism and church-planting, then "Christian witness overseas" is a far better word to express what the so-called "nonprofessionals" do. I want to make it very clear from the outset for reasons already given,[1] and for further reasons given below, that it is the personal conviction of the author that the importance of the nonprofessional missionary has been vastly exaggerated to the detriment of the main task of the churches, namely, to plant more churches in lands where there are none or only very few. Especially in student circles, perhaps, we have been guilty of giving the impression that the college professor, businessman, or doctor who does Christian work overseas as well as earning his living, is in some way a more advanced kind of missionary than the old-fashioned "conventional," run-of-the-mill, less well-educated, Bible-pounding professional. This has been a serious error and has hindered effective missionary work in many instances, because people who might have made a notable contribution for many years as straight church-planting missionaries have made a much smaller contribution because they were trying to do two things at once, and in consequence did neither very well.

SOME OUTSTANDING EXAMPLES

This is not to underrate for one moment some outstanding pieces of missionary work which have been done by some out-

[1]See chaps. 1 and 7.

standing nonprofessionals. There are some countries where no
other kind of Christian penetration has been possible. Anything overtly Christian would have been crushed from the
first. The Muslim lands of West Asia are open only to nonprofessionals. I have been privileged to know some outstanding men in both Africa and Asia who, while working in secular
capacities as college professors or businessmen, have done an
outstanding work which has transformed the situation in the
country concerned. It is such men who have initiated university Christian fellowship groups, started young people's camps,
Scripture Unions, evangelical libraries, and much besides.
They were outstanding men whom the Lord used to do an
outstanding job. In situations where the organized churches
already existing were in grave danger of becoming dead and
formal, a new generation of highly intellectual and gifted
national Christian leadership was brought into being through
the work of such men. It is probable that there still remain
some situations where, perhaps on a smaller scale, that kind of
job needs to be repeated again and again.

It is probably significant that many of these outstanding
examples come from countries where English is the language
used in education and business, and so it could also be used for
personal evangelism and teaching the Bible. Often they are
countries formerly attached to the British colonial empire
where expatriates are still being employed in various capacities.[2] With independence these openings are not nearly so
numerous as they were.

Outstanding work has been done by outstanding men. That
is the point. These men would have been outstanding in any
situation. They were able to be efficient and effective in two

[2]Historically, British colonial authority has not been overly sympathetic
to missionaries, and in many cases there was frank hostility to Christian
work as being bad for trade. Sir Stamford Raffles was a notable exception, and during the very short period of British suzerainty in Java before
it was handed back to the Dutch, he became the patron and first president
of the Javanese Bible Society in 1814.

fields at once, doing an amazing piece of Christian work as well as being extremely competent professionally. If they had been toothbrush salesmen, they would still have done the same. Outstanding men may be used to do an outstanding work. But not many of us *are* outstanding. The tragedy is that good Christian men of lesser ability have tried to emulate them and failed to do two things at once. The more ordinary, mediocre class two-type of men can do one thing at a time extremely well. Unfortunately, if they try to do two things at once in missionary situations, they either do a lot of Christian work but fail professionally or, more commonly, in spite of early promise, they advance professionally but achieve very little from a strategic Christian viewpoint (which, after all, was why the whole idea was so warmly supported to begin with). In some instances it has proved to be an unsatisfactory diversion—not a missionary by-pass but a complete by-pass.

THE NONPROFESSIONAL'S ADVANTAGES

The greatest advantage of being a nonprofessional is that one is freed from any suggestion that one is an active Christian because one is paid for it. In some countries it is sometimes unjustly thought that people who make money out of religion, whether they be professional Buddhist monks or Muslim teachers, are many of them unprincipled rogues who make a soft living out of other people's gullibility. We have already seen how Buddhist priests in Japan recite the *sutras* to the spirits of the dead to prevent them from troubling the living.[3] To put it crudely, the priests have a monopoly on the undertaking business. Although it is recognized that some of them do this work in order to gain merit, it is commonly believed that many do it just for the money. Christian missionaries and ministers may so easily be viewed in the same light. Simple people do not know of the more favorable financial

[3]See p. 26.

prospects which have been surrendered in order to become a missionary. That it might be regarded as sacrificial to come and live in their country and share their life is not a viewpoint calculated to appeal to a national, even if it occurred to him! The nonprofessional is thus very definitely in an advantageous position in this regard. If he speaks of Christ, he does so because he wants to, altruistically and without any suspicion of financial gain or personal advantage. This lends a real effectiveness to his testimony.

Second, the nonprofessional may well have access to circles which are closed to his more humble missionary brother. He will probably be more socially acceptable, not only to diplomatic and military people of his own nationality, but also in the upper strata of national society. And if he is an academic, he will move easily in the more intellectual circles as well. Thus he may have key openings denied to all but the more remarkable and most gifted missionaries. In this sense, especially, such work can be very strategic, especially if such a person is a gifted personal worker.

Third, by virtue of his respected position in the university with his students, or by virtue of his position in the country's international society, the influence of such a man is potentially greater than that of the humble missionary who may be something of an odd character socially, avoiding the social life from personal inclination as much as financial necessity.

Fourth, the missionary who returns home in middle age for health or family reasons may have some difficulty in finding satisfactory employment. From the viewpoint of material security the "nonprofessional" is undeniably at a very considerable advantage, not only in the salary he receives and the standard of living he is able to maintain, but also because he is able, as a rule, to maintain his position professionally, and perhaps even to enhance it as a result of gaining wider experience abroad. At any point he can usually return home and continue in his profession, should changing political circumstances, health, etc., make it necessary for him to cut short his work overseas. Whether such considerations should ever be the decisive ones for a consecrated Christian is another matter, and it would seem important to be certain that all such motives have been carefully sifted. If a man opts for a nonprofessional status because of security or financial advantage (unless support of relatives is involved), rather than because of the clear guidance of the Lord, this will tend to mar his witness. For there are also considerable disadvantages in the nonprofessional sphere which should also be honestly faced.

SOME SOBERING DISADVANTAGES

First, there is the difficulty we have already mentioned of doing two jobs at once. For the man of only average ability, the probability is that one of them will not be done properly. Even in these days of air-conditioning, there is a considerable difference in the amount of work a man can get through in the temperate climate in which he has grown up, compared with the very different situations in more tropical regions where a great deal is new to him. Most people find they just cannot carry as heavy a work load. It is of course easier for the single person than for the married man who needs to give time to his wife and children once the hectic business of teaching hours are over. It needs to be honestly faced that, however idealistically we may plan to do a great deal of strategic Christian work, we may discover that the whole pressure of life is against us. If we are working in a country which is closed to Christians from overseas who want to come as professional missionaries, then we shall need to labor on, however difficult we may find it.

Second (and this is the other side of the coin of access to circles closed to professional missionaries), the standard of living which we are expected to maintain may in fact cut us off from the greater bulk of the people. In some situations, indeed, the restricted but exhausting social life expected of those in diplomatic service and in business may also effectively cut us off from national believers. The very standard of living which is customary for foreigners sets the nonprofessional would-be missionary in an entirely separate compartment from those among whom he is trying to work.

Third, there is the serious problem of language. We may have the highest intentions of intending to learn a vernacular. If, however, we are frequently moved from one tribal or dialect area to another, particularly in some agricultural and forestry responsibilities, we may be completely frustrated in our desire to communicate. Even in countries where better-educated people do possess conversational English, quite frequently they do not possess a religious vocabulary. In such situations, the nonprofessional is certainly able "to make friends," but may then have to call in a professional missionary in order "to influence people" using the national language. We are not denying that in such countries the nonprofessional is often able to make many fine friendships with influential people which one hopes might result in their finding Christ. But so often, unfortunately, that desired goal is never reached.

It must be strongly emphasized that, just as opportunities for ordinary missionary work vary tremendously from country to country, so also do the opportunities for nonprofessionals. In some countries they may be able to do a remarkable and strategic work which no one else could do. In other situations they are nice to have around, but virtually prevented by the language barrier from doing effective work. They then usually end up by working chiefly among other foreigners.

A SUGGESTED SYNTHESIS

There are, however, other possible solutions to this dilemma. In countries where the language poses a formidable barrier, some remarkably fine work has been done by people with a good academic training who have first joined a missionary society working with national churches in a particular country. Perhaps the church is well rooted in a peasant environment, but so far little impact has been made among intellectuals. In this way, the "professional nonprofessional" is able to get to know the country, learn the language, and fully understand the church situation. From a position within the country, he is also often able to understand more clearly which are the truly strategic openings. After gaining an adequate grasp of the language, it is then possible to look for university and college teaching positions. In these jobs the ability to teach in the national language is very important. In many instances one may not even have to apply; when a person's qualifications and credentials are known and he is found to possess the ability to express himself clearly in the national language, positions may be offered even before he is ready to accept them.

For example, one pharmacist of my acquaintance spent his first term working at a mission hospital and gaining a good command of the national language. On furlough he was able to complete doctoral studies and returned to a key teaching post a major capital city where there was no active Christian witness in any of the universities. By the time he had completed his next tour of service, he had been used to bring into being small Christian groups in several different departments of the university. This is a pattern which seems increasingly appropriate in countries where a national language must first be learned. By such a course, the "professional nonprofessional" is able to get the best of both worlds. He is not just one of those bluff, genial, well-meaning Christian men who is unfortunately unable to speak the language and seems rather clueless, but someone who has served an apprenticeship with the national churches and can communicate effectively, using not only the language, but also the thought patterns of the people.

Personally, I believe this approach is a most helpful correc-
tive to the overemphasis on nonprofessionals which has, in my
opinion, been such an unfortunate sidetrack from the main
task in recent decades. More than this, the national churches
and the missionary societies desperately need missionaries of
academic training and high intellectual capacity in order that
they may carry out their work effectively. Such an arrangement
ensures that there is no dichotomy between the "professional"
and "nonprofessional" type of approach. It means that the
free-lance work of the academic is thoroughly integrated into
the work of other Christians, both national and international.

COUNTING THE COST

To some, the prospect of abandoning key university appoint-
ments in the prestige universities at home seems bleak. Surely
to do this would be a waste of one's training in burying oneself
in some distant land in a university of indifferent academic
standards. Just supposing that one needed to return in middle
life, one could scarcely hope to take up where one has left off.
To this, of course, the straightforward reply is that this is so in
the case of every other missionary. The way of discipleship
is not just for those with low intelligence or for Bible-pounding "professionals." Christ's word that "whoever would save
his life will lose it" is equally true for all Christian disciples,
however well intellectually endowed or academically promising. I cannot do better than quote Dr. Kenneth Pike, professor of linguistics at the University of Michigan:

> Another dilemma may face the younger scholar: often he
> feels that his training implies an eternal commitment to a par-
> ticular task—(or at least a life-long investment, which at the
> moment may seem long enough!). But the tug at his interests,
> or compassion, or the available places for work, may appear
> to lead to the loss of the investment in that training. He finds
> it hard to realize that many scholars have shifted fields and
> jobs with gain—not loss. The crucial personality invariant is

the permanently moulded character of the trained man—not the few concepts temporarily in his head.

YOURS YOU

How

        can I change my job?

Lose

        the years of work invested?

Fail

        my dreams of role fulfilled?

Dump

        all that?

Moses —

        (Orator-Engineer)

Daniel —

        (Area Specialist)

Paul —

        (Expert in the Law)

Training,

        "Used"? ?—*Why?*

Yours —

        degree, talent, this-and-that;

You —

        psyche, mind, guts

God —

        turns shepherd heart to King.

Role —

        grows from *man*—not robot.

Training Call.[4]

[4]Kenneth L. Pike, *Stir, Change, Create* (Grand Rapids: Eerdmans, 1967), p. 54, used by permission.

CLOSED DOORS

All that has been said above in pointing out the disadvantages of nonprofessional missionary work should not, of course, be taken as any discouragement in countries where no other approach is at present possible. The views expressed are the result of experience and observations made in countries where both approaches are possible.

There are, however, several countries where the door to Christians from outside has now been more or less closed. Entry permits and visas for professional Christian workers are not available. In such situations, the nonprofessional is the only one who can make a contribution. The same limitations as have been outlined above will of course still operate, but some kind of Christian contribution from outside is better than none. There are, of course, other countries where the door has not been open to missionary work for some time. Perhaps the door was closed by Islam many centuries ago. There are also opportunities in other lands where different regimes may be totally hostile to a Christian viewpoint, where the church is underground and missionary work unthinkable. To have an official link with a missionary society is fatal to our gaining entry.

In such situations, we should not allow ourselves to hide behind the concept of "a closed door." We must remind ourselves that 150 years ago, the doors were all closed. There were still bulletin boards banning Christianity in Japan when the first Protestant missionaries quietly entered and went on with the task of Bible translation. One notable nonprofessional, Dr. William Clarke of the Massachusetts Agricultural College, was appointed to go to Japan to help found an agricultural college in the northern island of Hokkaido. Although Bibles were forbidden, he deliberately took a stock with him to give to the students. When it was suggested to him that he would not be allowed to teach Christianity, he replied that in that case he would not feel free to teach anything else. Courage and strength of character won the day. When Clarke left after six months, all the students of the first year in the new college had signed a "covenant of believers in Jesus." Through the testimony of students in the first year, several in the second year were converted after Clarke had left, including the notable and outstanding Christian leader, Uchimura Kanzo. Clarke is still remembered in Japan for his parting words to his students, "Boys, be ambitious for Jesus Christ," although the most common quotation sadly omits the last three words.

In Korea again, there had been terrible persecution by the brutally antichristian prince regent. There is, of course, the amazing story of Bishop Mutel who went twice, secretly by night, once to baptize the regent's wife, Princess Mary, and once to administer to her the Lord's Supper. It was in this kind of difficult situation that in 1884 Dr. Horace Allen went to Korea as physician to the American legation and to the other diplomatic groups in Seoul. Dr. Allen was in fact a missionary under the Presbyterian Board, but could not have entered the country apart from his appointment to the legation.[5] To men like these, "closed doors" were a challenge. More modern examples cannot be quoted for obvious reasons. It is certainly in the critical task of performing the seemingly impossible and getting through a "closed door" that the so-called nonprofessional finds his greatest usefulness.

It is good to record that the increasing flexibility of various Bible colleges and other theological institutions means that it is possible for such "nonprofessionals" to gain some necessary theological training in short courses which can be obtained in long summer vacations or on a sabbatical leave. Some missionary societies have excellent practical arrangements whereby nonprofessionals may be "field partners" with no official rela-

[5]See Allen D. Clark, *History of the Korean Church* (Seoul: CLS, 1961),

tionship, and yet able to share and benefit from the fellowship and facilities of the missionaries.

Perhaps then the distinction between "professional" and "nonprofessional" is not really so significant after all. It does seem to the writer, however, that Paul is more usually called "the apostle" than "the tentmaker." There is little doubt which part of his work has survived the longest.

9 Facing the Future

MANY OF US have heard people talking as though the day of missionary work were almost over—and questioning how much longer missionaries will be relevant. This kind of talk can be very unsettling if one is considering serving overseas, and makes one think twice about it. It is a good point to discover just who is talking like this.

Sometimes those who talk in such vein are theorists; it is unusual to hear someone who has been a missionary talk that way. This could be merely because missionaries have an inflated idea of their own importance, and thus always feel that more missionaries are needed to replace them, or it might be because they are familiar with the tremendous needs that exist.[1]

Personally, having seen the great need for evangelism and church-planting and, even where a national church does exist already, for church-pivoted outreach, I feel angry, even furious, with those who theorize in this way (sometimes on a basis of one country only) when we know from personal experience of so many places where international missionaries from East and West are still desperately needed.

Two main reasons are usually advanced why missionaries will not be required much longer. The first is the closing-doors syndrome, and the other, the idea (a correct one) that the national church is taking over in many countries, and therefore missionaries will not be needed much longer (a mistaken one).

[1]See pp. 23 ff.

CLOSING DOORS

If one looks at things in a historical perspective, one thinks rather differently. Just over a century and a half ago, nearly all doors were closed. Such doors did not open readily. Carey got into India only by living in the Danish colony of Serampore. Adoniram Judson could not get into India. Henry Martyn and others could not get in as missionaries (owing to the opposition of the British East India Company) but only as military chaplains. The first missionaries in Siam could find housing only within the grounds of the Portuguese embassy. The Dutch authorities in Indonesia (the East Indies), while prepared to encourage churches for Dutch and Eurasians, did their utmost to prevent work among the Javanese, impounding the tracts and the New Testament produced by Brückner.

Yet, courageous Christian men slid quietly through whatever cracks there were. A hundred years ago, as already mentioned, there were still bulletin boards banning Christianity in Japan, but a few missionaries were quietly translating the Bible and teaching. Korea has been open for missionary work (and that also just a small crack at first, with notices banning Christianity still in evidence) only for some eighty-odd years. Other countries have opened far more recently, and others are still in the process of opening. The closing of some doors then in China, Burma, the Sudan, and the reduction of the vast total of missionaries in India should not be taken to herald the end of all missionary work everywhere.

When doors close, they often close rather spectacularly with a loud bang, as with China. When they open, they open quietly and nobody talks very openly about it for fear of prejudicing the opportunity.

Closing doors in one country means opening ones in another, as trained missionaries are available to serve elsewhere. A partial closing of the door to India means missionaries set free to work among Tamils in Malaysia, or Muslims in the Middle East. The closing of Burma meant missionaries available to reach the Shan people in west Thailand.

Even if some doors are closed, it needs to be realized how many doors still stand wide open. If the whole of mainland Southeast Asia were to be closed tomorrow because of communist advance, there would still be nearly 300 million people in the Asian islands—Indonesia, the Philippines, Taiwan, and Japan.

Perhaps the most important reason for not being panicked by closing doors is the biblical injunction of our Lord, and the biblical example of the apostles. "When they persecute you in one town, flee to the next" (Mt 10:23) seems a sound theological reason for believing that overseas evangelistic opportunity will continue until the Lord's return. "This gospel of the kingdom shall be preached in the whole world for a witness to all the nations, and *then* the end shall come" (Mt 24:14, NASB); that is, the terms of the Great Commission are binding until the time of the Lord's return. Paul and Barnabas fled from Antioch to Iconium to Lystra, from Lystra to Derbe, and they were chased out of each place; the doors were closed. But not very tightly, for we find them returning to these cities in turn once more. There is a pattern here for Christian workers.

In response to the closing-doors scare, then, look at it in a longer historical perspective. Look at the theological precepts and remember that those who watch the clouds will never sow. If missionaries had waited to go to China or anywhere else until it *looked* safe, they would never have gone. All through Chinese church history there have been wars and rumors of wars, revolutions and riots, yet missionaries went in quietly, and obeyed Christ's command. This will, I believe, continue until He returns.

The National Church Takes Over

We have already discussed the national church in chapter 2,[2] but one fact needs to be pointed out again. While in some countries there may be an active and effective national church at present, and the need for missionaries—except in certain specialist categories—may be less than it has been, yet in many others the national church, being pitifully small, is not able to tackle the task of evangelizing its own countrymen without help from the international church. The theorists may urge that the only value of the missionary today is to be an "ecumenical symbol." Certainly nobody worthy of his salt wants to be a symbol merely for the appearance of the thing. In Japan, for example, the so-called United Church (which accounts for perhaps roughly half of the Protestant Christians in the country) finds it difficult to know how to employ missionaries. Men with doctorates in theology have even been assigned to teach English conversation classes. Many missionaries attached to that church have gone home frustrated, because there was "no work" for them to do—and that in a country with ninety-nine million unconverted people! The fact is that the majority of missionaries work with evangelical churches outside the "United" Church, and are pioneering in totally unevangelized rural areas or the rapidly spreading dormitory areas of the cities.

This is scarcely a new story. The missionary Guido Verbeck, as we have seen, wrote that no more missionaries were needed in 1889—over eighty years ago! At that time the church was doubling in size every three years. But they were not to know that, following on a wave of antiforeign feeling in 1890, the church, contending with theological modernism on the one hand and with nationalistic militarism on the other, would in fact begin to shrink in size from that year onward. By the

[2]See especially pp. 32 ff.

time the militarists were finished in 1946, the country needed to be almost totally reevangelized from scratch.

This is one illustration that should prevent us from assuming that "the national church" will necessarily finish the evangelization of this generation, even if it should in theory. It was for this reason that Augustus Pieters, in his book *Mission Problems in Japan,* argued that missionary societies should retain a measure of independent initiative in order that they might be free to evangelize where the organized national church for some reason might lose its vision.

In the nature of the case, churches and denominations and fellowships of churches tend to weaken and to fossilize into institutionalism, just as did the churches of Asia in the first century (see Rev 2:4; 3:15). When churches grow cold they cease to send missionaries. Whenever there is revival, then there tends to be a fresh spate of missionary activity. By such means, then, the missionary-sending churches always remain the thrusting, growing edge of the church militant.

COLONIALISM AND PATERNALISM

A historical perspective is very important. Some people's ideas have progressed little beyond the topee-topped, strait-laced, and cholera-belt-defended "missionary" of the mid-nineteenth century. We often fail to realize that the change and development in secular history have been paralleled by corresponding changes in the church. In the colonial period it was scarcely surprising that missionaries, as men of their own time, were distinctly paternalistic in their attitudes. There was a considerable chasm in standards of living and in education between the missionary and the disease-ridden, illiterate people to whom they went. Christian compassion demanded that medical help be given, and that people be taught to read the Bible for themselves. Necessarily, then, the day of the great denominational missions was also the day of institutional mission schools and hospitals. Although, as has been suggested, colonial and imperialistic powers were often opposed to Protestant missionary work because it might hinder trade,[3] missionaries were often only able to enter because of a territory being under the protection of their own nation's colonial office. Inevitably the attitude of such missionaries was paternalistic. A worker among the Sumatran Bataks wrote: "The national workers are the arms, but the missionary is the heart"! The missionary built his house on the hill, with school, church, and hospital grouped around it, and few saw any problems in this "compound" mentality.

At the expenditure of many lives, then (however fashionable it may be, let us not sneer at these men of great pioneering courage), the churches were founded. Hindsight shows that there were real drawbacks. Inevitably such work was missionary-centered and compound-centered, rather than church-centered, but it was the natural product of its own generation.

NATIONALISM AND "PAULINISM"

From the turn of the century onward, however, secular history began to take a new turn as the different nations began to work toward political independence. This developing consciousness of "we nationals" and "those foreigners," which of course had always existed, now became increasingly insistent in its demands for political autonomy. The churches could scarcely avoid the corollary: if we can run our own country, we can certainly run our own church.

Thus, just as early missionary paternalism was the natural counterpart of secular colonialism, so the move for political independence saw a corresponding adjustment in missionary attitudes. In 1890 the veteran China missionary Nevius spent a couple of weeks in the newly opened Korean field of the

---

[3]For a detailed consideration, see Stephen Neill, *Colonialism and Christian Missions* (New York: McGraw Hill, 1966).

American Northern Presbyterians. What became known as the
Nevius plan for foreign missions gave these aims:

1. Let each man "abide in the calling wherein he was
found," teaching that each is to be an individual worker for
Christ, and to live Christ in his own neighborhood, supporting himself by his trade.

2. Develop church methods and machinery only so far as
the native church is able to take care of and manage them.

3. As far as the church itself is able to provide the men and
the means, set aside the better qualified to do evangelistic work
among their neighbors.

4. Let the natives provide their own church buildings, which
are to be native in architecture, and of such style as the local
church can afford to put up.[4]

Whether the church grew because the method worked, or
the method worked because the church was growing, is still
being hotly argued. But the fact is that missionaries would
arrive and teach inquirers for a week, and leave them with
Bibles and catechism, promising to return six months later to
baptize those who were ready. Then they would move on to
another village. On returning in six months, they would find
not only candidates for baptism but some natural leaders with
marked teaching gifts emerging and ready to be appointed as
elders. These were encouraged to attend the midwinter Bible
school for further instruction and this later became the Pyong-
yang Seminary. Instead of waiting for mission boards in the
home lands to grant money for buildings, use of a local house
meant that if numbers got too big, it was not too hard to knock
down a wall and enlarge the building. Even though this church
was under antichristian Japanese domination from 1905, it
grew steadily, and when the Korean War came and Christians
from the evangelized north fled south, the gospel spread in the
south as well.

[4]Allen D. Clark, *History of the Korean Church* (Seoul: CLS, 1961), p.
86.

Roland Allen was also a China missionary. In 1912 he wrote
Missionary Methods: St. Paul's or Ours? in which he pointed
out that missions had become missionary- and mission-centered:
"A mission station is a stationary mission and a mass of station-
ery." Paul had rarely settled anywhere for longer than three
years, and after ten years of work could declare that there was
no more work for him to do in the whole of what is today modern Greece and Turkey (Ro 15:19, 23) .[5] He appointed national believers to take charge almost at once (Ac 14:21-23). Mo-
bility, not mission stations, is the key. Trust that the new believers have received the Holy Spirit, just as we have. Make
converts, teach converts, appoint elders and move on. Such an
approach to missionary work was the obvious counterpart to
the desire for increasing political independence. Sadly, not
everyone listened, and in many cases the old methods prevailed
for years after they might have been abandoned. You will still
find relics of wrong attitudes. A Japanese friend of mine used
to recommend Allen's book to missionaries who came out expecting to "head up the work" in the fifties and sixties.

The method of "Paulinism," then, stressing national responsibility, was a real step forward in church-planting. But it also
has some disadvantages. It is fine as a pioneer method in an
unevangelized country. At a later stage, however, it merely encourages multidenominational chaos. Each denomination es-
tablishes a branch in a new area to compete with those already
there, because of the theory that this church will then plant
other churches.

The theory is that churches which are self-governing and
self-supporting will become self-propagating. But what if they
don't? The older churches in many older sending countries have
been self-governing and self-supporting for centuries but may
never have propagated very much, except biologically through
their children. The fact is, in days of nationalism, churches

[5]An area which needs reevangelizing today, please note.

are ready to be self-governing before the leaders have been Christians very long. Financial independence of foreigners is also easy to encourage. Sadly, many churches attain both these desirable stages, but fail to become self-propagating. This means that the missionary task still remains to be done all over again.

Third, this method seems to work better in a rural community than in detribalized and depersonalized city complexes. Modified, it ought to work in those situations, as we shall see, but the world is still changing fast.

Urbanization and Mass Communications

The world is still changing, but the changes now are sociological rather than political. Missionaries who still use the good old nineteenth-century methods are finding that they often seem to draw less and less response. Take Japan as an extreme example of urbanization. It is certainly an unusual one in that Edo (the precursor of modern Tokyo) had a population of over a million in 1800 before London had more than 600,000.

In Japan, urbanization began before the Industrial Revolution, rather than being one of its consequences. In 1951, 40 percent of the Japanese population were still in rural agricultural areas. Fifteen years later, only 11 percent were still so employed. Every year a million and a half people or more, mainly youngsters, abandoned the country in favor of the city. In some rural areas 95 percent of those who left school also left the towns where they had grown up, for work in major cities.

Trying to establish local congregations in such centers is like trying to catch water in a sieve. Ministry to young people is often seen as one of the best ways to establish a congregation, but if nineteen out of every twenty converts among young people leave the district, founding a church takes you twenty times as long as you might have hoped in a more stable society.

In fact, urbanization is not really such a hindrance, provided work is done in the growing cities to which these people move. These newly arrived additions to the city, with no roots, cut off from the traditional shrine and temple, are more responsive to the gospel than either country-dwellers or those who have lived in the city for generations.

The problem is to know how to make contact with them. A little thought will show that evangelism becomes increasingly difficult when it is based upon the urban residential area because, in moving from the friendly countryside, the detribalized city-dweller is increasingly isolated from neighbors. The TV set isolates from those next door, the car insulates a man from greetings in the street, and if he lives in an apartment, there is no longer the backyard fence convenient for a short chat with the man next door, or a long gossip with the woman next door after hanging out the laundry.

Using the traditional nineteenth-century approach, the busy missionary gets his posters and handbills printed, sticks up his posters, and distributes his handbills, using a good deal of Christian money and Christian time in the process, expended in the service of the Lord. Then in the evening, after (with police permission) a blast around the neighborhood on a public-address system (definitely more twentieth-century!), he waits hopefully outside the hired hall or tent erected on a vacant lot. The response has been increasingly meager in recent years. Those who come are either brought by friends or fished in rather reluctantly off the street at the last moment; the posters and handbills do not seem to bring much return. Why this poor response?

Because at just that time of evening in a Japanese city there may be as many as eight television channels in action, three of them in color. I heard recently that the city of Bangkok now has three channels (one of them in color with a second on the way). People who want to know things these days simply do not as a rule attend meetings in public halls or tents; they listen to the country's greatest experts speaking to them on television in the privacy of their homes.

The great problem in the urban metropolis in these days of mass communications is to get a hearing for the gospel at all. How can we get the ear of non-Christians in order that they may hear the gospel? The day when the pith-helmeted big white chief arrived and the curious indigenous population gathered to hear his words of wisdom, if such a time ever existed, has certainly gone forever now. It is so easy to accuse people of indifference or of being resistant to the gospel when what we really mean is that our methods are not appropriate to communicating with busy twentieth-century, urban-living man with his television set.

The probability is that television will be universal by the end of the next decade. Japan is already finding new markets, but with a wristwatch-size television receiver going into production, the changeover, even in more remote areas, will probably take place sooner rather than later.

The Christian Response

The church has tried to respond to many of these changes. For some the answer has been methodology: specialization in the ministry of literature, radio, and students' and young people's work. But there is always the danger that the enthusiast with a particular bee in his bonnet will go overboard in thinking of the value of that particular approach. Even if a tract is placed in the hand of every individual, it does not really mean that they read what they are given or understand what they read. Even if every individual hears a radio program—undoubtedly a useful way of giving people the opportunity to hear—it does not necessarily bring churches into being.

University student work has been my own particular pet "bee" in my missionary bonnet—the importance of reaching the future leaders of the country, its intelligentsia and elite with the gospel. Actually, however, there are so many university students these days that not very many of them are elite, and still fewer are really intellectuals! Moreover, while good work can be done in getting students together to witness and work for the Lord on their campuses, it is obvious that the best Christian students are those who benefit from the teaching of a good local church. In provincial centers where the local churches may be few, small, and weak, student witness is often consequently weak. Where there is a strong, effective local church, then the student witness flourishes as well. Certainly after students have graduated they desperately need good local churches into which they can be integrated.

The various specialist arms are thus auxiliary to church-planting, and not substitutes for it. Radio work depends upon having Christians to follow up interested listeners and upon the existence of churches for them to join. Literature work depends upon having Christians to distribute tracts and to buy the Christian books and to get them out among non-Christians. As already mentioned, distribution is always the big bottleneck. A new missionary may arrive wanting to teach in a Bible school. But there is little point in starting a Bible school unless there are first of all churches to provide gifted young people for training, and which will then support the new workers when they have been trained. The local church is always the essential and primary unit, and however excellent the auxiliary ministries, they are only auxiliary to the main aim. And while they may influence and bless the churches through their ministry, the success of their own ministry depends very much upon the dedication and growth of the local churches.

Do not misunderstand me. We need the very best possible ministry, through literature, radio, and television, and to students and young people, that we can get. Too often such ministries are far too greatly molded on their Western counterparts: books and tracts are translations of proved English-language books, often of a highly devotional character. Radio programs are too often models of the traditional Western-type of Christian program with solos (sometimes still in English!) and calculated to appeal more to traditional Western nonconformist sentimentality than to the ignorant non-Christians needing something more contemporary.

If radio evangelism is so traditional and hidebound and so often lacking in creative originality, one wonders how Christians will communicate on television. After all, a radio ministry can be carried on with a minimum of equipment; basically a preacher and a tape recorder are enough for the kind of thing which has been run-of-the-mill. But television will hardly sustain twenty minutes or more of close-ups of ministerial physiognomy in full spate of eloquence. The medium demands other ways of presenting truth. The church will have to recruit people with training in mass communication, ingenious minds of the kind which might compose skits, comic poems, or university revues. They must not only communicate verbally but visually, so graphic arts and cartooning are needed as well as musical skills. The gospel has to get across in this new medium. Christians should take this seriously: 99 percent of households in Japan have television, and other Asian nations are not so far behind. Bangkok had 39 percent four or five years ago, and in Singapore, Kuala Lumpur, etc., television is widespread not only in wealthier Chinese homes, but in the villages as well. In South America people may not have shoes, but may have television!

Another significant factor is the increasing availability of video-tape attachments so that a TV set may not only use televised programs from the studio, but also (much as a record player or tape recorder) play audio-visual reels plugged in and appearing on the screen. Such tapes will be purchased from stores or borrowed from libraries. This means that not only can people watch their favorite programs, plays, comedians, etc., over and over again, but also that well-prepared Christian programs may not only be broadcast by buying time on commercial channels (an expensive project), but also used over and over again in countless Christian homes.

The bottleneck is not the technology, or really the money, but Christian creativity and imagination in gospel presentation. The old illustrated children's talk may be modernized and technically improved, and then be used to reach adults! Comparatively few missionaries will need to be involved in such an approach, and those who are involved will need to be highly qualified and gifted, full of ideas, and able to train national Christians to produce material to reach their fellow countrymen.

THE MAIN TASK

As has been repeatedly emphasized, the main job to be done is to lead men and women to Christ and to build them together into vitally active, growing, and multiplying congregations. This may best be done by cell groups in high-rise apartment blocks, offices, and factories. When everyone else is multistory, the churches can hardly continue to build single-story buildings in pseudo-Gothic as though that had very much to do with New Testament Christianity. House and flat churches are more likely to meet the needs of the growing cities.

People these days are reacting strongly against the impersonal nature of modern society—where everyone is just a cog in a vast machine, part of a vast computerized society to be dropped into the correct slot. Impersonal mass methods of communication will have their place in a widespread making known of Christian ideas, and especially the more negative ministry of breaking down prejudices and common misconceptions. Whether warfare is conducted with catapults and arbalests, cannons and Gatling guns, or sophisticated atomic weapons of terrible destructivity, infantry will always be needed. Similarly, however advanced becomes the technology of mass communication (pocket telephones, satellite universities, and libraries available at the touch of a television knob), the basic work of gospel communication will always be person to person. In such situations, particularly where national churches are still weak, the international missionary force will always need to be available for personal work and a congregation-building ministry.

MERGERS

In a chapter on "Facing the Future," it seems worthwhile to point out one of the other interesting missionary trends of our day. Initially Hudson Taylor and other founders of interdenominational, so-called "faith missions" were reacting against the institutionalized denominational missionary societies. New missionary bodies have multiplied, however, in a way which has sometimes suggested more an ignorance of what is already being done by like-minded evangelical Christians than the absolute necessity of forming a new missionary group. The situation has deteriorated to such an extent that there is now a vast multiplicity of overlapping, and sometimes even competitive, missionary societies often possessing nothing, except their names and origin, which really distinguishes them from others. In Japan, for example, there are no less than 120 foreign mission boards at work, over half of whom have four or fewer members on the field. While most of these bodies are drawn at present from North America, which provides the major share of the world's total Protestant missionary force, one trembles to think what will happen if there is a corresponding formation of missionary societies in each of the Asian, African, and South American countries with the aim of sending missionaries to each of the other countries of the world!

In the homelands, there is a multiplicity of rather inferior mission magazines and a thoroughly uneconomical multiplication of councils and committees which take up the time of busy Christian men. In recent years there has been an encouraging move among missionary societies to put their houses in order. There have already been some mergers and there will almost certainly be more. Such moves may well be resisted by the more conservative among us, but should be greatly welcomed if it means that overhead is cut down at home, less Christian time is taken up with marginal matters, and more time and money can be used for essentials. Such greater cooperation should also enable missionary societies to better serve their missionaries on furlough, the children of missionaries being educated at home, and retired missionaries. The churches would certainly welcome the possibility of fewer missionary societies and a few really good magazines, perhaps one representing Christian missionary work within a whole continent. Fewer, better-organized missionary societies would also mean a much closer relationship with the local churches at home, which is much to be desired.

On the field, again, closer working together would not only cut down overhead in the use of offices and equipment, but would also seem essential for tackling major projects such as mass communication, evangelism, and higher-level theological education in which few societies could really hope to make an outstanding contribution on their own.

One hopes that this decade may well produce many such changes and that, while this may mean the loss of traditional and well-loved names and sets of initials, they may well provide a more effective framework for Christian work than the existing random outcrops of sanctified individualism have permitted hitherto. This is certainly an interesting time to live!

PERSONAL ANXIETIES

It is possible that we may have our own personal fears
about our own particular future. Sometimes a potential candidate who is of the "What if—?" temperament may be fearful
of being found outdated and returning home in middle life,
unemployed with a wife and several small children to support.
A single person may wonder whether a job will be available
and whether professionally he or she has grown out-of-date
and unemployable.

One does not detect in Paul any anxiety about God's good-
ness and ability to provide for him in later years. He writes to
the Philippians from prison, "My God shall supply all your
needs" (Phil 4:19, NASB) and this was in the context of the
supply of his own needs, having learned to be content in every
kind of situation. "I know now how to live when things are
difficult, and I know how to live when things are prosperous.
In general and in particular I have learned the secret of facing
either plenty or poverty. I am ready for anything through the
strength of the one who lives within me" (Phil 4:12-13,
Phillips).

Nonetheless, we know from his other letter written to Timothy in his old age that he felt the lack of "the parchments" to
satisfy his mind, a need for "the cloak" to warm his body, and
Timothy's company to satisfy his desire for human fellowship.
In spite of the glorious testimony of "I have fought the good
fight, I have finished the course, I have kept the faith; in the
future there is laid up for me the crown of righteousness, which
the Lord, the righteous Judge, will award to me on that day;
and not only to me, but also to all who have loved His appearing" (2 Ti 4:7-8, NASB), one does get a picture of a lonely old
man in his prison cell.

The supreme answer to this kind of problem is the same
kind of faith as Paul's. But there are perhaps times when our

anxieties about the future are greater than our faith. Thus one can also answer this difficulty from a purely material viewpoint, that where governments make ample provision for the care of the aged, and where missionary societies operate superannuation and pension schemes, there is less ground for anxiety. Or, as has been suggested above, even if one door closes, and the area in which we have been working becomes closed to foreign nationals, a trained and experienced missionary is valued and can be redeployed elsewhere. If because of language, health, or age this is not recommended, the home churches also would value the experienced soul-winner and planter of churches in their own outreach. Similar problems and anxieties are of course shared in common with other people working in overseas countries. Even in one's own land there can be no absolute security of tenure, and many workers even in leadership and management in industry have found themselves outdated or unemployed. If you are really worried about this kind of thing, then perhaps you had better give up the idea of being a missionary at all.

Fears and anxieties we all have. This is normal. We wonder what kind of frightening world we have heading toward us. One thing is certain. Until Christ appears to wind it all up, in this kind of rapidly changing world, however difficult it may become, Christians must continue to fulfill their God-given commission, seeking to "win all sorts of men . . . by every possible means" (1 Co 9:22, Phillips).

As this chapter has tried to show, the shape of missions has been constantly changing as society has changed. But however much such changes continue, there is a job to be done. We need not fear that we shall suddenly find ourselves in some outdated occupation, left behind by the progress of mankind, like thatchers or blacksmiths, in a slowly disappearing trade. Man's "progress" technologically shows little sign of any progress morally. High standards of living and better education do not seem to bring men the happiness they seek. However the modes of living and working may change, there will always be a need for the churches to have their evangelistic outreach, their trained catalysts, and their pioneer assault groups.

Writing on "The seed growing secretly," R. S. Wallace says:

> God has been at work amongst men in a sovereign way all through past centuries, ruling in the hearts of His people. There are hidden spheres where God's will is done: there is an invisible network spread through the nations, growing and entwining itself in this world like a hidden mass of underground roots. We have heard much during the past years of underground movements, invisible organizations that work below the surface to undermine prevailing circumstances. They are deep secret, but they are powerful for the overthrow of existing governments. The Kingdom of God is in the midst of this world, working like an underground movement of cosmic significance towards a glorious future climax.[6]

We of the church of Jesus Christ are like such an underground commando group working quietly but effectively in person-to-person communication of the message of Christ, in order to spread the news of the coming King and His inevitable triumph.

[6]R. S. Wallace, *Many Things in Parables* (Grand Rapids: Eerdmans, 1963), p. 13.

10 Today: What Will You Have Me Do?

"IF YOU HAVE RACED with men on foot, and they have wearied you, how will you compete with horses? And if in a safe land you fall down, how will you do in the jungle of the Jordan?" (Jer 12:5, RSV).

There is a real danger that those bitten by a "missionary bug" will spend all their time thinking about the future and neglect the present. It was significant that the men whom the churches chose and sent in Acts were people who were already active in the churches.[1] Barnabas and Silas were both notable figures in the Jerusalem church, and even young Timothy was well spoken of, not only by those in his own church, but by believers in the next town as well.

If I am interviewing a candidate for the ministry at home or for overseas, I am not so much interested in what he thinks he might become, but rather in what he is already.[2] It is almost pathetic to find people enthusing about working in other countries when they have not yet done anything very much in their own. If a person cannot lead people to Christ in his home country, in his own home language, communicating in the common heritage of language and idiom, how can he hope to communicate in another country? The church which has not seen a conversion or adult baptism in its own congregation for ten years is unlikely to produce any potential missionaries. The same can be said about a student Christian fellowship

---

[1]As we saw in chap. 1, p. 13 ff.

[2]People have a remarkable knack of developing fresh interests, revealing hidden potential, etc., when they get abroad, and advance speculations are quite wrong because they relate, not to an actual field situation, but to books that have been read or talks that have been heard.

group which is merely a "Cave of Adullam" for Christians where few, if any, of the members have found Christ in the college or university. It is the home churches and Christian student groups which are praying for conversions, expecting conversions, and seeing conversions which are most likely to produce people with the necessary gifts for full-time ministry at home or abroad. If some individual has not already started to manifest and to exercise spiritual gifts, it is a highly dubious procedure to accept such a candidate in the hope that he may develop such gifts after he enters a full-time ministry or has begun to serve overseas. It is so much easier in one's own culture and language than it can ever be in another.

TODAY

If you ask about preparation for future service, the answer is "Today." "Go and work *today* in my vineyard," said the man in our Lord's parable. "Go and make disciples of all nations" is not a command about future behavior when you have been inducted as a minister or sailed or flown with some missionary society. It is an order given over 1,900 years ago, never rescinded and still in force today. No special guidance or authorization is required. The man who is not already obeying it *today* is unlikely to obey it tomorrow either. There is a glorious existentialism in the Bible. We are always thinking so much about tomorrow and the day after, that we often fail to enjoy today properly. The Bible is always urging us: "Today." It is so easy to dream about *future* ministry instead of getting on with the job now. The man who is likely to make a good future minister or missionary is the kind who is already very active in the Lord's work.

The trend in recent years to stress professional qualifications has often ignored this and, provided someone has professional training and experience as a doctor or nurse, accountant or secretary, apparently nobody is very worried about how much experience he has in direct church work. People may even arrive overseas who have never addressed an adult meeting, and whose experience of Christian work is largely confined to teaching in a Sunday school or attending a youth club! We want the kind of ministers and missionaries who have initiative, people who have started something—a Christian student group, a Bible class, an evangelistic coffee house, a Christian guitar group or a new type of pioneer outreach of some kind. If people are not leaders in their own land, they are unlikely to be accepted as leaders anywhere else, and unlikely to make much of a contribution. An active outreach in the Lord's service *today* is essential.

God Is Preparing Us

The Lord is often in less of a hurry than we are. As indicated earlier, we do need some younger-than-average missionaries.[3] But, nonetheless, other churches want mature workers. It was fourteen years from the time of Paul's conversion to the time of his departure with Barnabas from Antioch. Those largely "hidden" years were not wasted. God was preparing His instrument: tempering and hardening him, hammering him into shape, teaching him. Paul was learning about discipleship, thinking out his own theology so that it could be taught with simplicity and clarity. It is clear that from the beginning he was an active witness (Ac 9:20, 22, 28-29).

This idea is well expressed also in the Lord's words to Jeremiah quoted at the beginning of this chapter. The difficult experiences of the present toughen us and prepare us for the harder experiences to come. We need the ability to be victorious through failure as well as in victory, to come through the disappointment of failure and unfruitfulness as well as the elation of success. Abroad there will certainly be disappointment, discouragement in plenty, sustained trials through ill health

[3]See p. 59.

or personal sorrow. Some experience of such things now pre-
pares us for what we may have to face one day.

Some things that may loom large at present as particular difficulties in the way of future service—ill health, an exam to
pass, parental objection, first refusal by a selection committee—may all be the foothills which we must surmount by faith
now if we are to climb much steeper mountains later on. Most
missionaries find that, if it is hard to go out the first time, each
furlough may bring with it the particular test of our willingness to go again, whatever the personal cost. The once-for-all
crisis and the once-for-all surrender, beloved of some conference and convention speakers, is usually one that is likely to
need repeating often! Each fresh surrender strengthens the
muscles of faith for a greater surrender and devotion to the
Lord next time. There is a real need to bind the sacrifice with
cords to the horns of the altar.

> "Take my life"—he said,
> But in the busy days ahead
> Forgot and took it back again.
> If "Take my life" your prayer should be,
> Then make it plain,
> And as a living sacrifice,
> Once on the altar,
> Keep it there.

In all the things which happen to us, all the crises we pass
through, the Lord is working to shape and mold us as a potter
shapes his vessel, remaking the marred parts. So do not panic
if your determination to serve tomorrow is severely tested today. Without today's shaping, tomorrow's serving would not
be possible.

Tomorrow May Never Come

"You do not know about tomorrow. What is your life? For
you are a mist that appears for a little time and then vanishes,"

writes practical James. Probably the majority of the readers of this book have already seen a quarter or more of their lives pass away. It is good to ask ourselves how much we have really achieved for Christ so far, and let that spur us on to fresh service.

Jonathan might well have wondered why God chose David and set him to one side. He did not know, as the Lord did, that he was to die with his father, Saul, on the slopes of Mount Gilboa at the hands of the Philistines. If Jonathan had seen all his service as future—"after I become king"—he would have been a failure. It was as crown prince, in his gracious life and glorious relationship with his friend David, that Jonathan's greatness was revealed. This intensely lovable man, who claimed the loyalty of that nameless armor-bearer as well as the deep affection of David, was a success in the years of expectation, rather than in the years of fulfillment.

Borden of Yale was a fine, dedicated, missionary candidate, but he died doing initial study of language and Islamics in Egypt and never reached the Muslims in China. The value of his life was not the "tomorrow" of missionary service which never really began, but the "today" of running Bible study groups for non-Christian students, and leading contemporaries to Christ at Yale.[4]

A compelling reason then for the "today" attitude is to be found in the possibility that "tomorrow" may not come. "Blessed is that slave whom his master finds so doing when he comes" (Mt 24:46, NASB).

And if the Lord's coming is delayed, then there is also the coming of the Stranger as T. S. Eliot described it:

> Oh, my soul, be prepared for the coming of the Stranger.
> Be prepared for Him who knows how to ask questions. . . .
> Though you forget the way to the Temple
> There is One who remembers the way to your door:

[4]See Mrs. Howard Taylor, *Borden of Yale* (Chicago: Moody Press, n.d.).

Life you may escape, but Death you shall not,
You shall not deny the Stranger. . . .[5]

Somebody might have to write an obituary on you next year.
Such compositions may well be trite; what matters is the certainty of service rendered to Christ, rather than the well-meaning kind thoughts of men, which may or may not be deserved.

PROCRASTINATION

We all tend to put off today what will wait till tomorrow.
Theological students so easily spend their time dreaming of
what they will do when they are ordained, or when they have
a church of their own. The Bible is always concerned about
today. Zacchaeus was told that "today" the Lord wanted to
stay in his house (Lk 19:5). In evangelism we have all used
the words, "Behold, now is the acceptable time; behold, now is
the day of salvation" (2 Co 6:2, RSV)—probably out of context! But it is not only non-Christians but Christians who need
this warning to act now. "Today, if you hear His voice, do not
harden your hearts" (Heb 3:7, NASB). Often biblical commands in the imperative suggest a once-for-all action. "Strip
off the filthy old clothes . . . and jump into the fresh clean
clothes" (Eph 4:24, paraphrased). We think it is far easier to
take off the old ones bit by bit, and slowly exchange them for
the new. It is the same with intercessory prayer or wider reading; we are forever intending to start and always putting it
off. Thus we need to recognize this danger, and seek to be
now what we want to become tomorrow.

In missionary situations, opportunities are rarely handed to
you on a plate. If you are the only Christian workers arriving
in a town without a church of any kind, and without Christians, then you will have to look for your own opportunities.
Thus in your present situation—in your street or place of work
—pray for guidance and for opportunities, and then go out to

[5]T. S. Eliot, "Choruses from the Rock."

look for them. All the experience that you get today will be of great value tomorrow. The muscles of your faith will be strengthened by present exercise for the greater exertions of the future.

It is good to gain experience of a widely varying kind—not only concentrating on one line that one is especially drawn to— for often one needs to learn to apply oneself to some new kind of work or opportunity for which at first one feels totally inexperienced and incapable. Rather than always going to the same camp for boys from London's East End, or public school boys, or children at the seaside, look also for opportunities of learning to tackle something new and different. Evangelistic missions and city campaigns give opportunity for a variety of experience.

HABIT-FORMING?

In a former generation they talked much of GMT (Good Missionary Training), recognizing that just as soldiers are trained by a rigorous discipline to make them able warriors when the time of battle comes, so also Christian workers need to form good habits. Regular sleep and regular exercise produce a well-tuned-up nervous system and a body which is not fat and sluggish. It is not only the physical disciplines but the intellectual ones which are important: discipline in regular and systematic wide reading, making notes of useful quotations, ability to recall and to use what one has read.

The person who leads a highly irregular life, going to bed late, getting up late, casual over meals and eating, indisciplined in work and study, and exercising no kind of discipline on himself in settling on priorities, does not seem to be as effective as the person who has decided clearly on what he is aiming at, and then single-mindedly pursues those goals, pruning away those things which are unhelpful or do not contribute directly to the main aim in view. Ability to distinguish between the good and the better, the better and the best, is a necessary quality when there are so many possible demands, and constant choice has to be exercised to know which is the most important.

THE NEXT STEPS

While stressing, then, the importance of the present, and the danger of merely dreaming about the future, immediately we want to ask, But what should I do now about overseas missionary work? At some point I shall need to take positive steps to discover whether I am suited, required, and prepared to move out of the present familiar environment into the unknown and perhaps frightening future. It is just at this point that so many fall down; they keep on putting off any definite steps precisely because of a reluctance to step out of the familiar into the unknown. It is as well to recognize this tendency, and to realize that once one has stepped out into the unknown—it isn't!

Looking back now, I realize how deep and yet how ridiculous were my exaggerated anxieties about new and strange places, places which are now so familiar that I feel more at home in them than I do in my own homeland. They are strange and frightening no longer, but loved and familiar. One can have a deep nostalgia and hunger for the places that once seemed so strange and unwelcome. So it is good to realize that faith must be accompanied by "deeds," and that this means going out to what is new and unknown.

PRAYERFUL MISSIONARY INTEREST

Other parts of the world are less unfamiliar if you take all possible steps to discover all you can about them. Andrew Fuller describes how the young William Carey pored over current books such as the journal of Captain Cook's last voyage, and then entered the details on a large homemade map of the world. "He had drawn with a pen a place for every nation of the known world, and entered into it whatever he met with in reading relative to its population, religion, *etc."*

Joining a small missionary group is often a way in which to gain useful detailed information about particular areas. The different members of the group will take letters from different missionaries known to them, gleaning other news from the magazines of different societies and fellowships working in the same geographical area. This kind of sharing and mutual encouragement enlarges the knowledge and stimulates the enthusiasm of the whole group.

If you cannot find such a missionary prayer group to join, start one. At the same time do not focus upon too small an area too soon. When such missionary groups were started in Cambridge University in 1950 (there were about forty different groups praying for different parts of the world) we adopted as a slogan the sentence, "Something about everywhere, and everything about somewhere." That is, the Christian should have the widest possible interest in all that is happening all over the world into which Christ came, a truly worldwide concern. But, in addition to this, he needs to concentrate on a particular region, country or part of a country for which he will study and pray in detail. This can be a fascinating and rewarding kind of involvement through reading letters, articles, books, and magazines and then praying intelligently about the churches and the national and international Christian workers in that area.

INFORMAL CONTACT WITH MISSIONARY SOCIETIES

In addition to producing literature, most missionary societies arrange conferences for their friends and supporters, and these provide an opportunity to get a feel of the society, its traditions and ethos. It is good to attend such conferences without any sense of obligation, in order to find out whether you like what you see and hear. Such groups will not try to pressure you into membership or present you with a ticket to the other side of the world. They are as interested in trying to discover what you are really like as you are to find out about them. You will doubtless be on your best behavior too, so do not be content with merely accepting the "public relations" image which a mission may wish to give of itself. An impression can be given by the literature of a missionary group which bears little relation to reality. Some missions are still living in the colonial era from the viewpoint of identification or relationships with national fellow believers, or even in the dark ages with regard to their attitude to the emerging churches and national leadership. Do they really know what they are doing? Are they forward- or backward-looking? And is the forward-looking talk in the high-sounding publicity handouts in fact being implemented by anyone?

Get to them as they really are—their principles and their practice, their actual problems. Try to get close to their missionaries on furlough and find out what makes them tick, and what their real frustrations are. You could be misled by some incompatible returned missionary with a grouch against his group (you can read the other side of the story between the lines then) ; but if the missionary is really sold on his job, concerned for those among whom he works, realistic and honest about his own achievements, painting neither too rosy a picture nor too black a one, you will get a good idea about the kind of group it is.

This is another reason, incidentally, why it is good not to concentrate too soon on just one society. It is good to have some standards of comparison so that you get to know where you would feel most at home. Getting to know a missionary society is rather like a courtship; you get to know one another, and gradually either you change your mind, feeling this is not the girl or the group for you, or you become increasingly enthusiastic. And very frequently the thing is reciprocal; where there is an affinity, you feel drawn to a fellowship and they feel drawn to you, or you both become increasingly cool.

Be realistic and not just romantic; a hankering for the wide-open spaces, the great mountain ranges, the jungles or the tribes may be part of your call, but it may be quite misleading. Discover where the greatest need is, and where work needs doing that is really worthwhile and to which you feel drawn.

COMMITTING YOURSELF

Probably you will have talks with missionaries or mission candidate secretaries (who are usually not so much recruiting officers, keen to send out all they can lay their hands on, as objective counselors who will try to deflect the obviously unsuitable and encourage those who show promise). The conversation will usually be indecisive, unless they know you well or are so impressed with you that they feel strongly that you should be encouraged.

Finally, however, you reach the point at which you are prepared to write the decisive letter. Do remember at this stage that, while you can express willingness, it is up to others to assess your suitability, and one measure of the society is the degree of thoroughness with which this is done. Do not be put off if, having seemed rather keen to enjoy your company until now, they stand back now that it reaches the point of proposal, and start asking a lot of pointed questions: often sheets and sheets of questionnaires, medical forms, doctrinal statements of your own views. Do not let this put you off, however much you dislike forms. They really want to be sure that you are suited and fitted. After all, it is your life that is involved and they are only being responsible to the churches overseas, to their own supporters and to you as a person, in being as thorough as possible in their investigations.

But do not be too anxious; there never have been any perfect candidates. All of us missionaries are weak and fallible human beings, and they will be sympathetic with your being a normal fallible person too. There is no point in trying to hide our weaknesses and pretend that we are supersaints when we are not. We have not yet attained the goal, as Paul reminds us, and when we have done everything we are still unprofitable servants, as our Lord told us.

You may be somewhat uncertain in your own mind, or you may have a very deep-rooted conviction that the Lord has called you. But remember, as we said in chapter 1, that our subjective convictions need to be confirmed by the objective recognition of corporate guidance. This does not mean that selection committees are always right; they are often impressed if, after an interval of further experience and testing, we come back to them, asking them to consider us once again, and may then give a favorable verdict.

If, however, you are gently and considerately told that they think it would not be wise to proceed further at this point, then see this as part of the guidance of the Lord through His church. It is foolish to let this throw you into depression, or to questionings about guidance; remember that you came to express availability, and others would decide suitability. When there are so many possible open doors before us, the firm closing of one door may be very clear guidance to go through another. It does not mean that you should go off in a huff and never darken their doors again. Many of the keenest and most loyal supporters of some missionary societies are those who have applied and been rejected. Surely the interest in some part of the world, if it has been real, will continue. It is not only those who go as missionaries who are "involved," but also those who send them and stand behind them. Thus if "preparing to be a missionary" leads to being something quite different, realize that you had to start along road A in order that you might come to fork B and on to your present road C.

Becoming a missionary is the end of this book, but remember that it is only a beginning. It is like being a new boy all over again. Certainly you have experience and knowledge in plenty, but in some regards you are still a novice in terms of the new environment. You may think that, after theological study and missionary training, you know it all. In theory perhaps you do, in practice not. There is much more that can be said at this point.

Your parents are going to miss you terribly. Each time you go there is always the thought in their minds, if not in yours, that next time you come back they may have gone. So show your love, and do not be afraid to let them know how very much they mean to you. Often the biggest sacrifice is theirs in letting you go, in those later years of life when they so much need your company in their loneliness. They will miss their grandchildren too.

Your friends will miss you, and the real ones will remember you. Some will just drift away and lose touch, but many will be your true friends praying for you and supporting you all they can. Friends are a blessing, and the more you can involve them as prayer partners, team supporters, and the like, the more they too will be blessed in involvement with you in work overseas. So do keep them informed both by regular circular and personal letters.

Your home church is the most important of all. Throughout this book we have tried to stress its importance. Spend time with them before you leave, and take every opportunity of getting them involved and keeping them informed. A farewell meeting may be an opportunity that is offered, and it is wonderfully worthwhile if prayerfully and carefully taken.

The Most Worthwhile Way of Spending a Life

Finally, let me conclude on a positive note. I have tried to point out some of the possible difficulties to be faced, even if in the event they are often avoided. If one is imaginative, most of one's worst fears remain unfulfilled! Such reality is good if it means that we avoid having new missionaries arriving all starry-eyed, feeling gallant and glamorous—and then before long becoming extremely disillusioned. Somehow these missionaries today do not seem as saintly and as easy to live with as those in the nineteenth-century biographies! The pleasure of working with national churches is spoiled by their apparent lack of gratitude and appreciation. Those beautiful color slides never managed to convey the smells of the city, and were never taken when it was raining. There is a great deal that is tedious and humdrum in the life of a missionary; there is a great deal of heartbreak and disappointment, not least with one's self. The wonderful things never seem to happen where we are. One spends so much time just "plodding." One is always having to discover that "long-suffering" is just as much a fruit of the Spirit as "joy."

But there is one thing that I must say and which I want you to remember. There is no more wonderful way of spending your life if this is what the Lord wants you to do. I suppose the missionary's first term is the worst; one is still stumbling along in the language, and feels so utterly incompetent. I shall never forget toward the end of my first term of service in Japan returning one winter night from a small rice-growing village. I had preached in my stumbling Japanese to perhaps half a dozen peasants in padded garments huddled around a small charcoal fire trying to keep warm. But I had sensed God's help in my preaching and they had listened; some eyes were shining with a dawning understanding. I headed back through the ice-bound paddy fields with the frozen snow crunching beneath my feet while the river meandered sluggishly through the ice, and the moon shone brightly on the glimmering snow of the great volcano. And as I hurried home with a knapsack full of Bibles and hymnbooks on my back, my heart was filled with a great joy at the privilege of being a servant of such a

Lord. I was so delighted with the privilege of it that I posi-
tively skipped through the snow!

It has been worth it. Some of them have understood. It has
been worth all the study and slog of these unproductive years
just to have been able to preach Christ to these people even
once. I have preached Christ in a place where He was not
known, and what could be more wonderful than that?